Thinking Outside of the Box... and Inside THE BOOK

by Paul Durocher

Barzell Publishing House

DISCLAIMER: Any personal gains or accomplishments noted in this book have been purely by the grace and mercy of God in spite of myself and to the glory of Jesus Christ and His remarkable ability to continue to reach into human history to deliver us from the greatest peril of all, the peril of ourselves.

Supplemental study guides are available at www.durocherfamilyministries.com/resources for download and use with small group studies, men's, and women's ministries.

Copyright 2008 Paul Durocher All rights Reserved

This book may be copied for personal use or group study up to two chapters at a time. It may be quoted our used in other works and any use should give proper credit.

Additional Copies can be ordered at

WWW. durocherfamilyministries.com

Published by Barzell Publishing House

ISBN-13 078-0-9817766-0-6

Cover Design and Layout by Barzell Design Works

TABLE OF CONTENTS

Introduction..pg 3
Forward...pg 8
Acknowledgments...pg 10

PRIORITIES..pg 12
Understand how laying a foundation of right priorities can become a compass in our lives to ensure true success and happiness.

HAPPINESS..pg 24
Examine what true happiness is in the 'culture of our souls' and explore three road blocks that hinder the flow of God-ordained happiness into our lives and how we can overcome.

MARRIAGE..pg 48
Discover three keys to intimacy through overcoming differences and moving into true love and mutual enjoyment.

CHILDREN...pg 66
Examine the concept of children being a blessing from the Lord and practical ways to maximize the blessing of children in our contemporary culture. You may be in for a surprise.

EDUCATION..pg 80
Taking it to the next level; home educators will be challenged to think deeply about the hows and whys of the contemporary educational maze.

MONEY..pg 102
Follow one family's path of the Lord's provision and guidance in raising 12 children while starting and managing a successful business. Learn the principles of gaining wealth, good stewardship, and passing on financial knowledge to the next generation.

REST...pg 142
Discover how rest is the secret to personal fulfillment and increased productivity. Examine life-changing components of spiritual, emotional, and physical rest.

CONCLUSION: A CALL TO ACTION...........................pg.168

Introduction

For as the heavens are higher than the earth, so are my ways higher than your ways, and my thoughts than your thoughts. —Isaiah 55:9 KJV

Let no man deceive himself. If any man among you seems to be wise in this world, let him become a fool, that he may be wise. For the wisdom of this world is foolishness with God. —1 Corinthians 3:18 KJV

But the natural man receiveth not the things of the Spirit of God: for they are foolishness unto him: neither can he know them, because they are spiritually discerned. —1 Corinthians 2:14 KJV

These verses have long intrigued me. As I write I acknowledge to the reader that this book is indeed a record of how these verses have been implemented in my life since I first believed them in 1980 as a junior in high school. Like Abraham of old the realization of these verses has been a dawning experience growing over the years in their impact and subsequent results. Two words serve as guideposts in describing this journey of faith.

The first is *serendipity*. Quite simply, it can be described as a pleasant and wonderful surprise. This has been my experience as I have staked my life on these concepts. Let me illustrate.

Imagine if you will that you were going on a journey to visit a relative, an old and somewhat ornery aunt (whom we'll call Nancy), out of a sense of family duty on any given holiday, say around Christmas time. The visit is boringly predictable. There will be the niceties of a simple visit, some conversation about distant relatives long not seen, perhaps a little assistance with some household chores and after enduring the stuffiness of the room with temperatures ten degrees higher than any healthy human being could stand, one will begin the departure process and gathering the kids for the drive home. There will be a mild sense of fulfillment in bringing encouragement to a needy soul as well as a sense of self gratification for fulfilling one's familial responsibilities, but all in all *boring predictability* is a perfect way to describe both the event and the subsequent aftermath of internal emotions.

Unfortunately, this is the way most people live, in the realm of boring predictability—so plain, so bland, so tasteless, like hospital food served up for the faint of heart. *They go through life empty and longing for something more all the while following the script for boring predictability.* It is this sense of emptiness, this gnawing sense of "something is missing" that drives sane people to the insanity of such culturally common anomalies as Internet chat rooms (and worse), gambling addictions, fantasy, immorality, and just plain depression and emptiness. Deep down in our heart of hearts we scream, "There has got to be something more." Do we not often think *"Why is everyone living such fulfilled lives and ours is so boringly predictable and full of struggles?"* We see images in the media of people fulfilling their dreams and doing exciting things while we have average kids with more than an average share of difficulties and family problems.

This book is about breaking away from the script. It's about a new and exciting type of insanity that leads not to self-destructive behaviors and the resultant internal wreckage, but to the introduction of whole new vistas of thought and experience bringing fulfillment unimaginable through touching our Creator in a deep and practical way often forsaken today.

Let's suppose our visit with Aunt Nancy took a different turn. Suppose somewhere between the tomato soup, saltines, and tuna sandwiches and taking out all the trash that built up in the back hallway over the past month that Aunt Nancy made an amazing revelation. She presented you with a check for $275,000! You and your wife sat there awestruck thinking "How can this be happening?" Instantly the ramifications of this *now serendipitous visit* flash through your mind. Mortgage paid off. New car. Home repairs will be a slam dunk. A REAL vacation. Now all of a sudden the possibilities are endless! Whole new horizons of opportunities are opened up. Life is changed instantly and wonderfully.

That is what this book is about. It's about a new way of thinking and living so that *serendipitous events can happen at any moment.* The visit with Aunt Nancy is a once-in-a-lifetime, no, a never-in-my-lifetime event. "This kind of stuff happens to other people, not me." Have you ever felt that way? But there is a disclaimer for the reader.

What you are about to read is my story. It is a living parable of how these principles have worked out in my family. The principles are for everyone but there is a cost.

One day the disciples asked Jesus a question and they simply could not believe the answer he gave. Their thought was "this is impossible who could believe it!" To which Jesus replied "Not all men can accept this statement, but only those to whom it has been given." (See Matthew 19:11) So it will be with this book. It will not be for everyone, but it is my prayer that some will find hope and confirmation of the principles that the Holy Spirit is already teaching them because truth can only come from the Spirit of God revealed to the human spirit (2 Corinthians 2:14).

This brings us to the second word, **counterintuitive.** As these verses tell us, the ways of God are often opposite or at least very different from what our natural thinking would lead us to believe. *Often following the path to true fulfillment means* *denying popular thinking and even at times our own internal human intuition.* Indeed this book is about contemplating a "new approach" to life. Let the reader beware: Any implementation will be at a cost of risk, sacrifice, and certainly misunderstanding from family, church, friends, and the world around us at times.

The spirit of this book is not about being Maverick or being different for the sake of being different. Some will react to what they perceive to be a "Lone Ranger Syndrome," or perhaps the thinking that one is "holier than thou" for choosing a different path. Doing things differently will always bring misunderstanding. This too is part of the cost. To keep it in perspective, let's talk briefly about the payoff.

We must understand that we do not reap in the season that we sow. Our family plants our garden in May and June and we reap in August through October. There is always a gap between sowing and reaping in which toil and painstaking labor and often more painful—waiting—take place. This is why I am currently writing this book. After nearly 25 years of sowing and experiencing trials, hardships, misunderstandings, and numerous serendipitous events, the reaping of recent years has so excited my soul that I wish to share it with hungry hearts, those that long for something more.

There is a saying that goes something like "You can't argue with success." Or "nothing breeds success like success." Americans are enamored with success. Usually this means financial success and worldly accomplishments. (Most societies of the world are satisfied with survival but Americans crave success and achievement). Thus this book.

This is really a result of a recent dawning realization— these life-giving principles I "stumbled upon" in my youth have opened the door for a life of fulfillment and success that I didn't understand I had so longed for and are the *true* desires of our hearts. It is my prayer that God will use these concepts to bring personal fulfillment and lasting success for each reader. Further any personal gains or accomplishments noted in this book have been purely by the grace and mercy of God in spite of myself and to the glory of Jesus Christ and his remarkable ability to continue to reach into human history to deliver us from the greatest peril of all, the peril of ourselves.

Author's Forward

The intent of this book is meant to be a popular and practical hands-on book which demonstrates biblical principles in real life situations. It is not this author's intent to be scholarly or academic. It is intended to be an easy read and although the content of the book deals with faith issues, abstract ideas, and philosophical concepts I have endeavored to treat this as a story as much as possible and not as how-to book or technical manual, or even a theological treatise.

As a result I have chosen not to footnote or cite references. Bible references are generally included in the text for the reader's convenience and to connect the reader with THE TEXT, which is most important. When the Scripture is quoted the version referenced is usually included following the quote. Much of what is included comes by way of personal testimony and application. I have observed that there are three things we can do with a proposition: prove it, explain it, or apply it. The majority of the dialogue contained in this manuscript is applicational by design. Without a doubt discerning readers will wonder about the validity of propositions and others will desire more explanation. It is largely the assumption of the author that the foundational presuppositions of the book are already held by the audience and what then becomes the path traveled is how these truths can be applied in new and, at times, radical ways.

Lastly, readers are encouraged to dialogue with me directly as the author as part of the ongoing story concerning these truths. Like the book of the Acts of the Apostles which has no real ending because we recognize that in some sense, the story is still being written, so too it is with this story. None of this is set in stone and the clarification that comes from communication as well as the fellowship that comes from like-minded brethren is a welcomed experience and one in which it is my prayer that this book will facilitate. Do you have a similar story? I would love to hear it. If you think I am all wet, I welcome your comments as well. (Please, no hate mail.) My intention in writing is to open up my life and the heritage that the Lord has allowed my wife and me to experience with a broader segment of the Lord's body and encourage like-minded believers and those with hungry hearts for a deeper walk with him.

I can be reached at pauldmn@hotmail.com. My mailing address is PO Box 170, Grand Rapids, MN 55744. I

Acknowledgments

I would like to dedicate this book my wife Judy without whose devotion to the Lord and willingness to entrust her life to the Lord so whole heartedly, much of this testimony would not exist. Her direct sacrifices in allowing me the time to hole away and write this book alone are a testimony to her life of extraordinary devotion to Christ.

I also wish to acknowledge my three oldest children, David, Susan, and Daniel and particularly David for their part in the development of the story and the enduring of the trials of faith from which it came. You know how it is with the first born. They are basically the guinea pig for the whole family experiment and these guys are awesome. Like their mother, their willingness to follow me as I have sought to follow the Lord has been a faith stretching exercise. Like Isaac of old this has not been some kind of academic exercise, but their lives have literally been laid down to demonstrate the principles of this book. Without them there would be no testimony, no results, and no book. It's difficult to be an Isaac when you are lying on the altar with your hands tied and wondering what's going on. These older ones have spent years there and have patiently served our family and their Lord without thought of personal gain. Their sacrifice has not gone unnoticed or unappreciated and I offer it as that which is worth of emulation by young people today.

Priorities Chapter One

The principles in this book really flow out of a loose but deeply embedded sense of priorities. If one were to read, understand, and apply every one of these principles and not develop the priority structure that served as a foundation for all, one would reach some measure of success and encouragement but would ultimately be experiencing defeat or frustration in several areas.

If our goal is total success in all areas of our lives, this must flow out of a sense of right priorities.

IT'S NOT ABOUT ME

The first priority principle is: *It's not about me*. Contrary to what our natural instincts might tell us, fulfillment in life comes from serving others and building a life that brings pleasure and fulfillment to others. Let me illustrate.

I recently met a business man from a foreign country who built his life around building a successful business. We were at a tropical island and he stopped there to refuel his plane and was taking a day to unwind while flying between countries (and of course taking advantage of the low fuel prices while there because there are significant wells there). There he sat at the twilight of his life, alone. Rich, successful, and alone. What is the point of a beautiful sunset if there is no one there to share it with? We are social creatures and even if we are single, our heart desires someone else there to say, "Wow did you see that?"

I have a friend who is a doctor. Not only a doctor, but one who came from a fairly affluent family. They are not the Rockerfellers by any stretch, but grew up skiing Colorado and taking real vacations (which I define as any vacation in which you don't go visit relatives). They have been very generous to us. Why? Well, not only do they love the Lord and His people, but also because their lives are enriched by sharing their fun times and special occasions with us.

They recently went skiing and packed four of our kids into their large van to go along with them. Upon returning I thanked him for taking the day off and driving, and was truly grateful for the sacrifice of his time and personal involvement with my kids. He replied, "No problem; my kids had a way better time with your kids along."

We all can understand this. It's a lesson I like to teach to my three-year-old daughter Melanie. I look right at her and tell her "sharing is fun… it gets you friends." She just looks up at me almost in unbelief. You could almost hear her thinking to herself, "You mean if I give this toy to my sister, *I'm* gonna be happier?" "Yep, that's right." Meeting needs in the lives of others brings us immense inner joy and pleasure and having an "others focus" is a foundational priority for a successful and enriching life.

I am not saying that we all need to go out and give away all we have, or go on the mission field to a third world country, I am simply saying that we need to have an others mentality in all that we do. We don't need to create special relationships or situations where we can begin this priority focus, we just need to start right now with all the many people God has already placed in our lives.

We can start with our spouses and children, then extended family, and co-workers, employees, supervisors and the convenience store clerk at the local station. Like the ripple in the pond, let the concentric circles of care and concern for others begin to engulf everyone.

+++

Now, we must notice that this chapter on priorities does not start with a list. In fact, you'll find little by way of lists in this book. It would be easy to say "OK men, here are our priorities: God first, the Word second, family third, church fourth, work fifth, etc. Perhaps if you've been in the kingdom you've thought in these types of terms or heard sermons in similar tones. The problem is that cookie cutters don't work in real life. They can be good benchmarks and general guidelines, but just when you think the formula is applied right, you make the wrong decision and people get hurt feelings or worse.

The priority of Others Orientation must begin as a desire and a prayer in our hearts. It then receives the critical application in our lives as we allow God to lead us by his ever present Spirit, the Holy Spirit in each individual situation.

It's like driving a car. In the beginning we need to focus on all the individual parts of the process and after a while we can zip along adjusting the radio, eating a pizza and talking on the cell phone all while changing lanes during rush hour. We've nearly forgotten the rules or at least become quite unconscious of them because a bigger element is now in focus. In our driving illustration it may be the purpose of our journey, the company we are keeping, or the conversation in progress. So it is with this process of focusing on others.

Begin by praying a simple prayer,

> *"Lord help me to think of others the way that You would want me to."*

We're not looking for big leaps, just little leanings—leaning our hearts in the right direction. Can we imagine what this planet would be like if men started becoming less selfish?

If we started thinking in these terms:
- What are my wife's needs today?
- What one thing could I do today to help her?

- I wonder what my daughter is thinking about lately?
- What is her biggest fear?
- What bad series of unfortunate events caused my cranky neighbor to be such a crank?

We have to acknowledge that we men are especially selfish. It is our selfish desires that cause us frustration and anger and to hurt those around us in so many little ways, and big ones too. This is such a clear priority principle. Paul spelled it out for us in Phillippians 2:3-5 (NAS):

Do nothing from selfishness or empty conceit, but with humility of mind let each of you regard one another as more important than himself; do not merely look out for your own personal interests, but also for the interests of others. Have this attitude in yourselves which was also in Christ Jesus.

Revolutionary! Thinking of others as more important than yourself! Looking out for the interests of others; in a nutshell, having the same attitude as Jesus did when it comes to thinking about others and relating to them in practical ways that demonstrate "I care about you," and "you matter to me."

For me this means asking one of my construction laborers, "How are you Pete?" and really meaning it! And asking about his live-in girlfriend, and did his kid get over his cold last week. Maybe it means offering him the last good seat when we sit down to lunch on a jobsite. It's just serving in little ways that say "you matter," even though I am the boss and the owner of the company, your family matters to me and your immediate comfort, a decent seat at lunch (admittedly a stupid little thing) is something I thought about.

It's not about me. If I get happiness and encouragement and even some fun and special things in life, it's all a bonus. Something I really don't deserve but God gave it to me anyway. How can we have this others focus?

A mindset such as this can only come from one thing — aligning my heart and mindset with that of the Lord and of his indwelling Holy Spirit. We can only do this as we experience the sufficiency of his presence in our lives. When he becomes the source of all life and godliness then we are full of the abundance of the riches of his glory, then we can abound in his fullness toward others. (We will look at this concept of abounding in fullness as the book unfolds since this is foundational to all Christian living.)

+++++

WALKING DAILY IN FELLOWSHIP WITH GOD

As we pray this little prayer we run smack into the second priority principle: learn to walk with God daily in moment by moment fellowship.

Scripture tells us that

- Adam walked with God in the cool of the day in the Garden of Eden.
- Abraham was a friend of God.
- Enoch walked with God and he was not, for God took him.
- David was a man after God's own heart.

Walking with God is really what this book is about. I mean REALLY WALKING WITH GOD. Thinking outside the box in the sense that we make a conscious effort NUMEROUS TIMES PER DAY to pray something like this:

Okay God what do you want me to do here? What are you trying to say to me in this situation? Lord how should I answer this question? Lord I'm going to turn the radio off on my drive to work today so we can just be together and enjoy each other's company. I want to tune into you to know what you want me to think about today. What is your will today in my life?

In a nut shell, it's putting God first. So you ask "if it's putting God first why is it second on the list?" The reason is because we begin with people and the stimulus of our five senses. We begin life by cutting and hacking and banging and dragging our way through life and somewhere along the way we learn about God. Hopefully we come to the realization that *He is* and that the complexities of life and human relationships are more than we can bear and we cry out to Him for help. This is the call of salvation for each of us. Usually by this time we've landed ourselves in quite some measure of human misery, whether it's relational, financial, or just plain loneliness, and we cry out to God to help us and deliver us. We begin to learn that He is capable and present, that He loves us and will come to our aid, at times it seems, when we need Him.

Someone once nobly said, "Stop the world, I want to get off!" If only we *could* stop the world and fix everything in our lives and then turn it back on again and pick up where we left off. The problem is that we can't. We still have this human stuff going on all around us as we seek to put God first in our lives and learn to walk with him. So as we go about our lives, going to school, making money, getting married, raising kids, we are encountered by a great priority, to put God first in our lives.

Consider the great words from Deuteronomy known as the Shamma. These words were memorized by every Hebrew and literally written on the scrolls that the more devout Jews wore on their foreheads in later years.

And thou shalt love the LORD thy God with all thine heart, and with all thy soul, and with all thy might. —Deuteronomy 6:5 (KJV)

I am not going to dwell on this priority because I am assuming most people picking up this book have already come to grips with this as a priority *at least in principle* and have experienced some measure of success in attempting it. It is my prayer that those who wish to deepen that desire will be able to do so as a result of this book in perhaps more practical ways. I hope as a result of this book one will be able to think more creatively about some of these things and allow God to bring one to new levels of experience in walking with him.

Before we leave this matter of priorities, we must consider Jesus' words in Mark 12:29-31 (KJV):

And Jesus answered him, The first of all the commandments is, Hear, O Israel; The Lord our God is one Lord: And thou shalt love the Lord thy God with all thy heart, and with all thy soul, and with all thy mind, and with all thy strength: this is the first commandment. And the second is like, namely this, Thou shalt love thy neighbour as thyself. There is none other commandment greater than these.

So in a nutshell we see from the Lord the two priorities of life: God and people. Loving God and serving others. Jesus has a way of getting the fluff out of the mix. God and people. The rest is just stuff; unimportant stuff in and of itself except, of course, as it relates to God and people.

Obviously we could write a book about these two great topics and the Lord reminded us that "on these rests the whole of the Law." In other words, all of life flows out of these two foundational priorities. We must not however move beyond this point until we've settled these two critical life issues.

1. Have we made a conscious decision to put God first in our lives by walking with him and living a life pleasing to Him in all that we do?
2. Have we made a conscious decision to live life with an others focus and seek to tame the beast of selfishness that resides in each of us?

How about praying a skeptic's prayer? "What's that" you ask? It's a prayer with a big if at the beginning that goes something like "God if you will help me to make a conscious effort to put you first, then in my heart of hearts I want to do it."

I love skeptics. Mostly because I am one. The skeptic *can't believe until he knows something*, but in his heart he *wants* to know it. So he prays the only sincere prayer in the world, "Lord show me."… Show me how it's true Lord… Show me how to believe… Show me these truths… Teach me how all this is supposed to work… Lord I cry out to you!" and finally … "If it's true and if you show me… I'll do it!"

I want to invite you to become a skeptic with me. Feel free to pray this prayer along with me as I have for this chapter, and for every other one in the entire book. You see, being a skeptic is safe. We don't make promises to God. We don't say "Yeah, I'm gonna put you first and I'm gonna be a servant to everyone, and I'm gonna give 20%", yada, yada, yada. No, we play it safe and leave the ball in his court. Lord if you will show me, then I will …. It's a great prayer because it moves us from presumption to faith. When God shows us something, then we move into the realm of obedience and an exciting walk with God. A serendipitous adventure.

This is the stuff that Moses was made of. (Fear not men, we are in good company) God had called Moses to do a difficult and impossible thing in leading 2.5 million people out of one country and into another whereby they also had to dispossess the peoples living therein. We're talking politics, whereby a person could easily be hated by thousands of his fellow countrymen while working his hardest, and war, whereby one could easily get stuck with sharp pointy objects, or worse yet, bludgeoned with dull ones. If there were ever a time when a skeptic wanted to be sure he was making the right decision it was Moses.

Please savor the following account of it:

12 And Moses said unto the LORD, See, thou sayest unto me, Bring up this people: and thou *has not let me know* whom thou wilt send with me. Yet thou hast said, I know thee by name, and thou hast also found grace in my sight.

13 Now therefore, I pray thee, *if* I have found grace in thy sight, *shew me now thy way, that I may know thee,* that I may find grace in thy sight: and consider that this nation is thy people.

14 And he said, My presence shall go with thee, and I will give thee rest.

15 And he said unto him, If thy presence go not with me, carry us not up hence.

16 For wherein shall it be known here that I and thy people have found grace in thy sight? is it not in that thou goest with us? so shall we be separated, I and thy people, from all the people that are upon the face of the earth.

17 And the LORD said unto Moses, I will do this thing also that thou hast spoken: for thou hast found grace in my sight, and I know thee by name. [Italics added] —Exodus 33:12-17 (KJV)

The bottom line is that Moses *needed to know* God's ways! He said "Show me and not only me, but make it clear enough that everyone else sees it too, or else forget it, I'm not going to go myself, let alone lead this people!" Wow, what a prayer!

What a skeptic! But, what an answer! God changed his mind and answered Moses' request and said he would indeed go up with the people and that he would give them rest, and that Moses found great favor with God.

Not only is this safe, but it leaves the responsibility where it belongs, with God. It was his idea to bring the people out. They were in fact h*is* people. This was not Moses' idea or mission. He was not some kind of megalomaniac. In fact, Numbers 12:3 tells us that Moses was the meekest man on the face of the earth. So this work had to be God's work and it had to be *demonstrably Hi*s. And so it was.

On an interesting side note, later, a squabble ensues as to who's the greatest. And as human nature would have it, the age-old power struggle ensued (I suppose not entirely different from the modern day church and family relationships), and Miriam and Aaron enter into a dispute about who really is the leader. There is not one word of protest or defense on Moses' part. But God steps in and *demonstrates* that Moses is *the* leader in a very dramatic and visual manner. He calls Miriam and Aaron out of the tent and descends upon them right there in front of everyone. He scolds them personally and vindicates Moses; then he departs and gives Miriam a leprous hand. Ouch. Pretty visible. Not something you can hide. Aaron cries out for forgiveness to Moses and asks him to forgive them and for her to be healed. Moses of course does exactly that, but then God does a strange thing. He says, "I'm gonna heal her, but I want everyone to know what she did in challenging your leadership. Send her outside the camp for 7 days with that there withered hand so she can think about who's really leading the show around here since she thinks she's so mighty." And all Israel sat still for seven days! That's right, nobody moved until everyone got the lesson. What was the point? A demonstration of God's power. Was this not an answer to Moses' prayer in

Numbers 12:16? *For wherein shall it be known here that I and thy people have found grace in thy sight? Is it not in that thou goest with us? So shall we be separated, I and thy people, from all the people that are upon the face of the earth.*

God made it known that Moses had indeed found favor with him and he separated Moses out from every other human leader.

So, my brothers, we want the same results from the same skeptic's prayer. We want God to show us His ways and separate us; make us a demonstration of His plan and power that it might be manifest *whose* we are. The result is that He gets the glory! It's not what we do, it's what he does through us! If there is any success or blessing, it's not because of our cunning or craftiness or wit or wisdom or good looks or our Ivy League degrees or our bloodlines or anything other than simple obedience to His ways. Whatever we possess then is "from Him and to Him" and His glory becomes our highest end. The high fives we experience when we do experience the blessedness of His presence then flow out in overflowing gratitude and resultant praise. The result is that He gets the credit and the glory. God is in the business of glorifying himself because he alone is worthy of glory. Furthermore, his glory he will not share with another. This is why he could use Moses and his face could literally radiate God's glory. Moses was so humbled and so utterly convinced of his own personal bankruptcy before God that he would never usurp the glory of God.

May I close this chapter on priorities by saying that this is exactly what God wants today; a man who longs to know and do the will of God. Is it no less precious today than it was 100 or 1,000 years ago? Is God no less powerful?

We are told that Henery Varely, a Sunday school teacher, said "The world is yet to see what God can do with a man whose heart is totally dedicated to him." To which a young DL Moody reportedly replied, "By God's grace I'll be that man."

DL Moody with little formal education and who, in the early years of his ministry and as a result of his Unitarian background, didn't even believe in the Trinity, became a world famous and greatly used evangelist.

In this thought we must also remember 2 Chronicles 16:9 which tells us "…the eyes of the Lord run to and fro throughout the earth that He might strongly support him whose heart is wholly thine." Yes, beloved in every age God wants to demonstrate His power to an unbelieving world. But to do that we've got to know his ways and be consumed with a passion for his glory. This is what the remaining chapters are about.

Happiness Chapter Two

Having concluded my initial thoughts on priorities, this book really starts with a discussion on happiness. Why happiness? This is a practical book and not a scholarly treatise. It begins where we are and seeks to bring scriptural solutions to bear on our problems and motivations along the way. So we start with priorities by way of foundational premises. Now, practically we move into a discussion on happiness as really a first objective of the human personality. Think about it.

A baby comes into the world and he does what babies do best, he cries. His parents being crowned with wisdom from on high do whatever it takes to stop this thing called crying. The grandparents and older siblings get involved. All become engulfed with the answer to one all-consuming quest: How can we make this baby happy? We try the bottle, we rock them, we lay them on their backs, no, on their stomachs, we wind up the swing, we sing to them, we bounce them, I have even seen parents take their infants for a drive in the car every night just to get them to stop crying and fall asleep. The quest of the human persona is happiness and it begins at an early age.

One need not be very creative about this as we look into the childhood years. The stereotypical child who is "spoiled" and who "gets his way" has succeeded in manipulating those around him into contemplating and providing for whatever makes him or her happy. Parents today are throwing up their hands in exasperation trying to make and keep their kids happy.

Move on into adolescence and the teenage years. No longer will toys, trinkets, and candy do to appease our desires for happiness. Now we want things like freedom, adult relationships, belonging, intimacy, privacy, and a whole list of even more destructive things than the candy and toys and Nintendo were. During these years the quest for happiness becomes more sophisticated and intentionally driven. It may not be quite so self destructive and may include noble aspirations such as academic success in making the grades or athletic conquests in various sports. All of these set the stage for the full fledged onset of adult happy-itis.

The whole world is looking for happiness. It is a cultural universal. We look in relationships seeking for that one special person who will bring us happiness. We look to our careers for that which we enjoy and energizes us. We look in leisure and entertainment activities for what we believe will bring us happiness. Of course for two thirds of the world, happiness is simply a quest for today's bread, clean water, and pennies worth of medication to soothe the pain of physical illness.

The sobering point is that every human being is in some measure involved in a quest for happiness, however they happen to define it. Blaise Pascal, the philosopher and mathematician, is reported to have said "All men seek happiness, this is without exception. Whatever different means they employ, they all tend to this end." Happiness as a cultural universal should not be met with much controversy.

If this is so, and we will assume it is indeed true, that all men seek happiness, then it must of necessity be something our Creator wired into our inherent makeup.

The opposite of happiness is depression. One might think it strange beginning a discussion on happiness by talking about happiness but we must first establish a critical contemporary cultural phenomena, namely depression, or the absence of true happiness. This takes many forms.

Being angry, feeling frustrated, self pity, feeling inferior, experiencing serious guilt or regret, experiencing constant defeat to lust, greed, and impurity, battling a sense of failure, living with excessive stress, facing the consequences of poor choices in the past, continual financial struggles, marriage tensions, feeling trapped in a job or unhealthy relationship, and the list could go on and on. Although these are normal experiences of the human personality as a result of living in a fallen world, my guess is that if any one or more of these things becomes a significant factor in one's life, say goodbye to happiness and say hello to depression. Maybe you live there.

It's hard to be happy when we are experiencing defeat and failure and the resultant consequences. Sure, we can cope. We can have a good time. Perhaps some of these have been your coping strategies.

- Watch lots of TV. It numbs the mind and causes one to forget all your troubles (at least for 30 minutes at a time).
- Drown yourself at work (at least you are doing something productive).
- Eat! A lot! Even if you are not hungry.
- Yell at your wife and scream at your kids. (Chances are some of what you are experiencing is their fault anyway.)
- Live in a fantasy world of immorality and pornography.
- Become obsessed with hobbies and exclude important people in your life while you do them.

There are a million ways we try to hide our pain and cope with the things that are eating away at our souls, but the truth is that these and other coping strategies only hide the depression—momentarily offering only a temporary sense of relief.

We all do this to some extent. After a tough day at work I really enjoy sitting down with the family or with the wife (that seldom happens) and watch a good movie. I don't want to talk;

I just want to veg-out, be entertained, and not think about any important stuff or make any decisions. A certain amount of this feeling is healthy; it's called unwinding. Hopefully we don't need a martini or a margarita to do so as culture would want us to think.

We live in such a fast-paced culture where we are forced to perform to excessive levels and the competition of capitalism drives the marketplace to sonic levels of stress-filled activity. I remember reading that Thomas Jefferson used to bring his violin along to play while he was writing the constitution and doing stressful political work to relax himself, take a stretch break, and appreciate the peaceful music. Unwinding is important, and I could probably write a book on this new *culture of exotic vacations and cruises* that were once a luxury and have now become standard fare for many working class couples and families.

Yet, in spite of all these coping strategies and unwinding times, many people still have not found true happiness.

Before we begin to look at success, happiness and blessing, and a life of faith in individual areas such as marriage, family, education, and finances, we first have to define a culture of the soul which ushers in true happiness.

We must have the right climate and weather conditions before we can perform even our most cherished activity. Golfing, going camping, attending a parade with the family, would perhaps be our favorite activities, but they could produce a whole lot of misery when undertaken in a thunderstorm.

This is what is happening inside of our souls. We undertake wonderful things that should make us happy but we end up miserable or in tensions.

- We get married only to end up fighting and experiencing constant misunderstanding.

- We go on a family vacation and end up in a fight with our wives or disappoint our children.
- We get that new raise or promotion, but somehow seem to still be coming up short at the end of the month.

Let's take a few moments and probe our souls and see what hindrances to happiness are lurking there and what can we do to eliminate them.

Before we plant the garden, we must remove the stones and sticks and roots. So too, before we look at the individual crops we would like to plant, we must tend the soil of our souls so the crops of a good marriage, mature and godly children, well-educated children, solid financial practices, including positive cash flow, etc. will find fertile soil to grow in.

Although there are many things that can trip us up and cut off the flow of happiness, three come to the forefront. These are the ones that clog up the pipes. More than anything else, they cut off the flow of one's ability to experience happiness. If any one of these things is operating in your life, I can guarantee you there are major areas of disappointment, frustration, and failure. The result: you are a less than happy person.

Let me first say that each item of the three is more than just a sin, it's an iniquity. A sin is a specific trespass, or a falling short of God's standard whereas an iniquity is a multitude of sins working together to manifest itself in many different individual sins. This will be come apparent as we discuss them.

PRIDE

The first thing is *pride*. Pride is the first sin of Satan, the Devil, Lucifer, the anointed cherub who was in the presence of God. (See Ezekiel 28 and Isaiah 14.) He declared himself equal with God and demanded worship of the other angels.

His chief sin was pride, and, as mentioned, it is an iniquity that encompasses numerous other sins. Let's look at the Psalms and Proverbs to get a practical handle on this thing called pride. Before we do, do yourself a favor. Table your preconceived notions of pride right now. Make a mental picture of pride, the big muscle guy with the tight tank top, or the guy with the big gaudy suit, both trying to impress someone. Make whatever mental picture you want—then throw it away! Look for the first time at what pride is as you read these words below and see if 'it's a pair of shoes in your closet (as it has been in mine).

The wicked, in the haughtiness of his countenance, does not seek Him. All his thoughts are, "There is no God." —Psalm 10:4 (NAS)

Pride is failing to acknowledge God. Pride is starting anything without God. Any time we don't seek God, we are dealing in pride. Jesus said "Without me you can do *nothing*" (John 15:5). Pride is failing to realize that strength and health are from God. All that we have comes from his hand. He has a purpose and a plan in all that we do and we must seek him. He delights when we seek him and is saddened when we don't. The truth of the matter is that we don't have to be a big, bad, foul-mouthed atheist who says, "There is no God!" to be guilty of pride; we only need to live like there is no God and to think that we can do fine without him.

This shows up in a thousand little ways if you think about it. This book is about being candid so I'm going to share one that I recognize and perhaps you can relate to.

All my life I drove old used cars. *Old* used cars. Often times *unwanted* old used cars. Before we went anywhere we would pray and seek the Lord. Just have a little family prayer asking the Lord's blessing on our journey, that he would prosper us on our way and of course keep the car running to get us there and back. Well as time went on we bought our first almost new car. At least one that we could trust and have confidence in, and wouldn't you know it, those little prayers became fewer and fewer. We used to do it as an example and encouragement to the children when we drove to town to go shopping. Surely big prayers were always offered up when we went to see Grandma 60 miles away because it was quite likely the car wouldn't make it! What's it like today? We jump in the car to go skiing in Colorado five states away and we're more concerned with remembering *what* to bring than remembering *Whom* to bring and invoking his blessing and purpose on our trip. I am overstating the case but I think you get what I'm saying.

So, when we don't seek God and things don't go our way, what happens? We get frustrated and frustration leads to anger, and anger leads to all kinds of strife and wrong decisions. So pride is a simple thing with huge ramifications; something as simple as not seeking God in all that we do. Let's keep looking.

The fear of the LORD is to hate evil; pride and arrogance and the evil way, and the perverted mouth, I hate.
—Proverbs 8:13 NAS

The concept of evil is introduced here in Proverbs 8:13. The first aspect of evil mentioned is pride and arrogance. We are told to hate evil. What evil are we to hate? Namely, pride and arrogance—first on the list. Not surprising. But what is the topic that all this hinges upon? The answer is found in the first part of the verse, namely, the fear of the Lord. If we fear the Lord, we will hate pride. If we have pride, we will not fear the Lord. The two are mutually exclusive and cannot coexist on one soul. Do you want to know if you have pride? Ask yourself, "What are the telltale signs in my life that I fear the Lord?

Am I concerned about his judgment of my sin and giving me a good spanking if I choose to disobey? Do I shutter at the offense of his majesty and holiness when men slander and blaspheme his name, or when I fail to glorify his name?

If I don't fear the Lord, then I am accountable to no one. I am my own boss, my own judge; I call the shots, and I say what I can and cannot do. 1 Corinthians 6:20 tells us *"For ye are bought with a price: therefore glorify God in your body, and in your spirit, which are God's"* (KJV). We belong to him! He is our Maker and our Master! Indeed we call him Lord. He sees everything we do and worse yet, he sits with us thinking every thought we think right along side of us because he is inside of us.

This perspective leads to humility, the opposite of pride. I realize that I am not even my own. I am just a servant of his. If I accomplish something it is *from* him and then *for* him. I am not to glorify myself, or live for myself; I am to live to glorify him and to live for him. Our next verse picks up on the relationship between humility and pride.

> *When pride comes, then comes dishonor, but with the humble is wisdom.* —Proverbs 11:2 (NAS)

One of the telltale signs of pride is dishonor. Pride will cause a man to do many stupid things from seeing who can drink the most at the local bar, to initiating a lawsuit to get back at someone. But the motivating factor in both our barbaric and sophisticated examples is pride. The net result is dishonor.

This word dishonor is translated confusion, dishonor, embarrassment, reproach, and shame in the Bible. Are these things a significant part of your life? If so then we must admit we have pride. It gets better.

We think we can sort of puff ourselves up a little bit and make ourselves look better in the eyes of others. Scripture tells us that when we do this, we will actually be brought lower in the eyes of others.

A man's pride will bring him low, but a humble spirit will obtain honor. —Proverbs 29:23 (NAS)

People can see pride in others... I've been guilty. My pride has caused others to react at times and I've been brought low. As a young preacher I was perceived as prideful and passed up for serving the Lord in a ministry that I felt I really wanted to pursue. On the other hand, when people see humility and level headedness, they sense wisdom and that person will be selected by his peers to lead and give direction to an organization, whether it's the church or in the marketplace. So the humble spirit will obtain honor.

Which most represents your life? Confusion, shame, embarrassment, and reproach, or wisdom, honor, and resultant responsibilities placed upon you because of your humble disposition?

There is one more little facet of pride we must reveal before leaving it and it's found in Jeremiah.

We have heard of the pride of Moab—he is very proud—of his haughtiness, his pride, his arrogance and his self-exaltation. 30 "I know his fury," declares the LORD. —Jeremiah 48:29-30

The king of Moab was very prideful and all the superlatives were used to describe him including haughty, arrogant, and self-exalted. Then the Lord says something very insightful, "I know his fury." What a revelation! Prideful people are furious or angry people.

Is anger a problem today? Is anger a problem with men today? Is anger a problem with you or me today? Does it characterize our lives? Does it infiltrate our relationships? If it does, we have pride.

As long as we have pride, and in this case manifested by anger, we are not going to be happy. We must take this inventory and rid ourselves of pride in all of its subcutaneous forms. That's a fancy medical term that means "under the skin." Any form of pride under the skin is going to cause a problem.

As a carpenter I get slivers with some degree of regularity. I've come to learn that the best time to get a sliver out is immediately, when you realize you get it. When you don't, you forget about it because it's so small and it doesn't really hurt; before long you hardly know it's there.... Until the next day. Waking up the next morning reveals a small aching feeling under your fingernail and you are reminded that you got that sliver the day before. So you pick at it for a few minutes, but it's in deeper than you thought and it's going to require some time and a special tool like a needle or razorblade to remove it and you've no time to mess with it now because life is going on all around you and you've got things to do and people to see so you tell yourself, "Ill get it later." You never do. By 3:00 your finger is throbbing every time you bump it the slightest bit. By evening it's nearly unbearable and keeps you up at night. It's red and tender all around the sliver which creates an even bigger problem. It's so painful at this time that it's too late to do anything about it. You've missed your opportunity. You don't have any anesthesia and you can't bring yourself to go digging into that puss-filled infected swollen mass to rid yourself of it. So you are left with one choice at this point, to go it for the long haul. You know from past experience that white puss will surround the lodged item and will begin to cut it off from the body. Over time it will cocoon itself with white blood cells and begin to die. It will be a slow and painful process that will take a long time. Oh how you wish you could have removed it sooner. But God's natural processes did what you were unwilling to do. So it is with pride.

Take an inventory and purpose to rid your self of pride. Recognize it for what it is, a grotesque clogging agent that stops the flow of blessing and joy and happiness to our lives and brings with it corruption and disaster.

So, pride is the first obstacle to our happiness. Let's look at a second obstacle to our happiness.

++++++

MATERIALISM

Materialism is the second iniquity that hinders the flow of happiness. Materialism quite simply is a focus on the material things in this universe to the detriment of the eternal and immaterial. I say eternal, because people are material, but they are in a different class than other material objects because they are eternal and also because they are immaterial, in that they have a soul and spirit.

Materialism is married to secularism. Picture them as head and tail of one coin. Secularism in its simplest form is a focus on the here and now, rather than on future rewards or, in the bigger picture, eternity and the things of eternity. The word secular comes from the Latin word *seculum*, meaning here and now. I will be using these terms nearly interchangeably. One has as its focus *things,* i.e. the things around us that we see; the other has as its focus *time and events,* i.e. what's happening right now versus the future.

When we embrace materialism, several happen. Things become more important than people. Temporal things, that is things related to time, become more important than things related to eternity. Or more simply, what I am doing today is more important that how this affects tomorrow or some point in the future.

This gets us into all kinds of trouble. In the materialistic bent we err in placing the majority of our energies in fulfilling our desires for things, whatever it may be. It could be the tool hanging on the shelf in the garage, the new cars, the boats, the vacations, the homes, the toys and trinkets, whatever. In the temporal it becomes what I am doing or want to do today versus the future. It could be the cigarette I want to smoke, the food I want to overeat, the alcohol I want to drink, the illicit relationship I want to be a part of, the immoral pictures I want to look at, or even my "right" to my Saturday golfing, fishing, or bowling. It says "I want to do what I want to do regardless of how it affects my future." Ultimately any time we sin we evidence temporal values.

I could give a hundred examples of these things but I think we all know what I am talking about. Let me give a few.

Decisions based on secularism:

- Missing your children's activities for personal interests and hobbies.
- Skipping church and fellowship opportunities for pleasure or entertainment.
- Choosing to overindulge in substances, including food, in spite of the future consequences.
- Taking a vacation today that you cannot afford.

Decisions based on materialism:

- Balling out your kid because he touched your things.
- Overworking to afford the extra things in life.
- Spending more than you can pay for (having debt related to items purchased and not related to food, shelter, and medical care. These are the only legitimate reasons for debt. More on debt

and finances later in our chapter concerning money.)
- Excluding people because of things.
- Trying to impress others with your home, clothes, cars, and stuff.

You see our aim in doing these things is that we think they will bring us happiness. In reality, they actually work in reverse against us. Overspending leads to debt that we need to pay back later and that thing we thought was so cool that we needed has lost its luster and no longer brings us the quick fix it did when we first got it. Overeating gets us overweight for which we need to make significant sacrifices later to lose those pounds or undergo the expensive heart surgeries and life-long medication bills.

Watching TV night after night only leaves home repairs and projects uncompleted and results in further needed repairs and a nagging spouse.

Failing to be at your kid's ball game, piano recital, or swim meet leads to strained relationships with the child later, not to mention serious regrets as we enter the twilight of our lives and realize that we've missed the truly significant for the insignificant.

We must always be on the lookout for materialism and secularism creeping their way into our decision making process. Someone once said that the price of freedom is eternal vigilance and so it is with the freedom of the soul.

One verse of scripture is exceedingly insightful in this regard.

While we look not at the things which are seen, but at the things which are not seen: for the things which are seen are temporal; but the things which are not seen are eternal. –2 Corinthians 4:18 (KJV)

The issue in all of our decision making processes is quite simply "what's going on here that I cannot see?"

What are the long range ramifications of this decision?

How will this affect me in two, ten, and twenty years, and in eternity?

How is this affecting the souls of men and women including mine, my wife's, and my children's?

The power of these questions and their ability to help us see the right choice of action is inestimable.

The best part about it all is that consistently thinking this way will open the floodgates for true happiness. Let's look at the third obstacle.

+++++

DEFILEMENT

The third obstacle, or log jamb, in the life of happiness is defilement. To be defiled means to be made dirty. There are actually several great terms that are translated defile in the New Testament. Let's take a look at a few of them.

The first word is *miaino* and it means primarily, "to stain, to tinge or dye with another color," as in the staining of a glass, hence, "to pollute, contaminate, soil, or defile." (Vines Expository Dictionary of NT Words)

The second is *moluno* which means basically to smear as with mud or filth or to befoul. It is used in the figurative sense, of a conscience "defiled" by sin (1 Corinthians 8:7); of believers who have kept themselves (their "garments") from "defilement" (Revelations 3:4), and of those who have not "soiled" themselves by adultery or fornication (Revelations 14:4).

Then there is a third, *spiloo* or *spilos*. Sounds like a spill in English and we all know what happens when red Kool-Aid or tomato sauce hits the carpet—a big stain. It does in fact mean "to make a stain or spot."

So to be defiled is to have some type of stain or blemish in our souls. A similar word is *miasma* which means a pollutant or contamination. God has so designed us that we are fine running equipment, and we can't run on garbage. How can we expect to experience happiness in life if we are filling our souls with things that pollute and corrupt and cause internal damage? One day I pulled up to the pumps at the gas station and I was talking on the cell phone and actually put gas into my diesel fueled pickup. It was an especially bad thing to do because I was completely on empty having driven with the low fuel light on for 50 miles, nearly a record. So even though I only put in a little, comparatively to the tank's capacity (I put in two gallons), it still affected the truck since it went right into the system and corrupted the fuel filters and fuel lines. After 70 miles and a $200 tow it was an expensive lesson. But let's not waste this lesson.

It doesn't take a lot of garbage to defile ourselves and usher in a great deal of unhappiness and lifelong consequence. You see, sin in the innermost being creates damaging effects, even though we may not realize it.

This is why David, the great king of Israel and man after God's own heart declared, "Thou dost require truth in the innermost being and in the hidden parts thou wilt teach me wisdom." He said these words as he was coming clean of the whole defiling incident with Bathsheba. David had lusted, fornicated, deceived, schemed, deceived again, plotted, murdered, and deceived again. What a mess. But because God loved David, he uncovered that mess and by the time things were over, David was bleeding all over. But in the end he was restored. He was forgiven; he was again blessed by God. The depth of his relationship with God soared to new heights as he experienced the person of God in new and wonderful ways. He could later say "How blessed is the man whose sin is forgiven, whose transgression is remembered no more." This would have a lot more meaning now that he had actually committed crimes that were worthy of death.

So it is with us. We've got to come clean of all defilement if we are to experience lasting happiness. Notice what the scripture says as we look at several passages.

Pure religion and undefiled before God and the Father is this, to visit the fatherless and widows in their affliction, and to keep himself unspotted from the world. –James 1:2 (KJV)

If God gives us this as a requirement of true religion, then to some extent it must be possible.

But with the precious blood of Christ, as of a lamb without blemish and without spot. –1 Peter 1:19 (KJV)

Notice here that Jesus Christ is the Lamb without spot or blemish. We are the "Christ-ones" and he desires us to be like him. That's where he's headed with this project of his. Jesus said in Matthew 5:48, "Be ye perfect as your father in heaven is perfect." Wow! Is this possible?

Wherefore, beloved, seeing that ye look for such things, be diligent that ye may be found of him in peace, without spot, and blameless. –2 Peter 3:14 (KJV)

Here is another passage. We are to be diligent to be found in him without spot and blameless. If it is the result of our diligent effort it must be possible.

But you say, "That's good for you; you are one of those godly types who grew up in a Christian family and aren't tempted and all messed up like I am". (I actually had someone tell me that once.) It is as though there is this belief that there are some people who are meant to be holy and free and others who will be plagued by relenting sins for their entire lives. Well, the truth is that those who know me best, including my wife, children, friends and extended family, really know better. So how do we get beyond defilement?

This subject could merit an entire book but let's reduce it to its most basic elements.

Confess any known sin in your life. Start by agreeing with God that a certain behavior is sinful. Tell him that you are sorry and that you want to live a life that is pleasing to him. Ask him to forgive you. Thank him for his forgiveness. Ask him now to help you not to do that sin anymore and MEAN IT IN YOUR HEART! Beloved, God is faithful. He will not allow you to be tempted more than you are able. He will provide a way of escape so that you can bear up under it. (See 1 Corinthians 10:13. Read this verse and write it down on an index card and carry it in your pocket.)

As we close this section on defilement we must look at a great example, that of the Apostle Paul in Acts 24:16. In this verse he says, "So I strive always to keep my conscience clear before God and man." That's it folks; striving to keep our consciences clear. This is what it means to be "walking in the light." None of us are perfect and we will never reach a stage of sinless perfection. Walking in the light is living in the fullness of the light that God gives you. It's your walk with him and not anyone else's. To be perfect means to be complete or whole. It means to live in the whole light afforded us.

When the Holy Spirit confronts us with defilement we confess it, grow in maturity and press on. Getting rid of the defilement may mean confessing and confessing and crying out and crying out and crying out until overcoming and winning become a life pattern. This may require getting help and having accountability, and there are a host of other strategies to assist in breaking and keeping free. Remember the price of freedom is eternal vigilance. Let him who thinks he stand take heed lest he fall.

So here we close this section on happiness. ***Removing the road blocks to experiencing God's ways by eliminating pride, materialism, and defilement will not only bring us happiness, but also prepare us to receive deeper insights into his ways.*** If any of these things are present, then our hearts cannot receive the Word since the soil is not prepared to bear fruit.

Lastly, before we leave this section on happiness we must consider Jesus' words in the Sermon on the Mount which repeatedly reminds us of the requirements for a happy life. They seem to ring afresh in this context as we look at them from the Living Bible.

6   Happy are those who long to be just and good, for they shall be completely satisfied.
7   Happy are the kind and merciful, for they shall be shown mercy.
8   Happy are those whose hearts are pure, for they shall see God.
9   Happy are those who strive for peace—they shall be called the sons of God.
10   Happy are those who are persecuted because they are good, for the Kingdom of Heaven is theirs.
11   When you are reviled and persecuted and lied about because you are my followers—wonderful!
12   Be happy about it! Be very glad! For a tremendous reward awaits you up in heaven. And remember, the ancient prophets were persecuted too. –Matthew 5:6-12 (TLB)

As we look at this list we see that pride, materialism and secularism, and defilement are the antithesis of the character qualities Jesus lays down for us. Meekness, humility of spirit, moral purity, loving peace, and having an eternal perspective are the positive side of experiencing blessedness.

It is of utmost significance that God is ultimately concerned with our happiness. So much so that he lays down a pattern for us to attain it. He wants it even more than we want it for ourselves. The key word here is counterintuitive. The means of attaining happiness according to Jesus may be just the opposite of our natural human inclination.

- Hedonism says, "If it feels good do it. It will make me happy."
- Materialism says, "I see it. I want it. I get it. It will make me happy."
- Secularism says, "Live for today and go for the gusto. It will make me happy."
- Humanism says, "I am the determiner of my own destiny; I call the shots. I do what I please to make me happy."

The world is crying out for happiness. If someone could patent "happy pills" I think he could find a market. The nearly six billion people on this ball of dirt are kicking and screaming, fighting and dying to find happiness. As we have said, it is a universal quest in the heart of man and God has created it thus. He leaves us not in the dark. He leaves our longings not unfulfilled. He meets us with solutions, answers, and best of all the internal motivations and power to do his will and experience the happiness that he so desires for us.

One more thing we must observe before we draw conclusions concerning happiness. Pride, defilement, and materialism (secularism) when turned loose in our lives all seek to effectively accomplish one very destructive goal—to eradicate the presence of God in our lives. These iniquities, or categories of sins, are effective in "cutting off the life of God" from our experience. We lose the manifestations of his presence with us although we know from Scripture that "He will never leave us or forsake us" (see Hebrews 5). With this being the case, we come via the back door to a remarkable but not surprising discovery: Happiness comes only by an experience of the presence of God in our lives. Consider the words of the psalmist.

> *Thou wilt shew me the path of life: in thy presence is fullness of joy; at thy right hand there are pleasures for evermore.* –Psalm 16:11 (KJV)

This is a most amazing passage. True joy and happiness come only from him. He alone can show each one of us the path of life, namely, that which brings each one of us the fulfillment of our soul's innermost longing. What is that? It is the joy that comes from the manifestation of his presence in our lives. Furthermore, it is the individual pleasures that come to us as a result of his presence in our lives. Notice that these flow to us from "his right hand." He is the source of our happiness, joy, and all of the individual "happenings" in our lives from which we derive pleasure. Let's look at another passage.

    7   How excellent is thy loving kindness, O God! Therefore the children of men put their trust under the shadow of thy wings.
    8   *They shall be abundantly satisfied with the fatness of thy house; and thou shalt make them drink of the river of thy pleasures.*
    9   *For with thee is the fountain of life: in thy light shall we see light.*
    10   O continue thy loving kindness unto them that know thee; and thy righteousness to the upright in heart.
    11   Let not the foot of pride come against me, and let not the hand of the wicked remove me.

12   There are the workers of iniquity fallen: they are cast down, and shall not be able to rise. –Psalm 36:7-11 (KJV—italics added)

The phrase being "satisfied with the fatness of thy house" is a picture of walking in fellowship with God. It envisions living with God, a great and wealthy king who alone possesses all things related to the fulfillment of our happiness, namely, the "fatness of thy house." God is full and overflowing with everything! His supply is unending and indeed this is the point of the following phrase, "thou shalt make them drink of the river of thy pleasures." Why a river? A river has a continual and unending source. It just flows by unceasingly. There is no thought of the origin of the water, only the presence of the water currently at hand. So it is with God's pleasures. His pleasures that he bestows upon us flow to us as a river. First we notice that they are THY pleasures. The things that please the heart of God and delight him become OUR pleasures. Secondly we notice that "thou shalt make them drink" of this river of pleasures. We are passive in the process. God "leads us beside the quiet waters, for his Name's sake." It is not something that we have sought out and prepared for ourselves. As we have delighted in him, and placed our trust in the "shadow of his wings" he has delivered us onto these delights and pleasures and "made us to drink of them."

The passage goes on to say "for with thee is a fountain of life." The Hebraic word pictures are effective in communicating to our souls. Like a river, a fountain is a gushing overflow of water under pressure that comes bursting up from the earth. It is powerful and its supply is abundant. So it is with God. He alone is a fountain of life. The word life here can be synonymous with happiness. From him comes all that which pertains to life, that which is life indeed.

It is further interesting here that the passage contains strong warnings against pride and unrighteousness (defilement) thus cutting off the flow of God's presence and blessing. Notice too, on the affirmative side, that these blessings come to those that "know thee" i.e. who experience his presence and hunger for his ways, and who are upright in heart, i.e. those who purpose to live without defilement and hunger and thirst after righteousness.

Finally, the passage closes with the results of iniquity, the very picturesque Hebraism of falling down and being unable to rise. What a picture of the very thing we have been talking about. Being overcome with the web of entanglements of individual sins that work together into a big ball of iniquity from which we are not able to rise and free ourselves.

As we conclude this section on the Culture of the Soul as it pertains to happiness we find then four principle ideas.

1. God is the source of all happiness first in his very presence alone in our lives as we delight in him and his ways.
2. All pleasures and individual sources of happiness come from him. Without him, even the good and the best things in life cannot be enjoyed.
3. It stands to reason then that anything that removes us from the practical presence of God in our lives and the life of fellowship with Him, cuts off that flow of happiness, which is life indeed, and for which our souls long.
4. If we were to summarize the whole of that which removes us from the presence of God we could see three overarching categories, namely pride, defilement, and materialism/secularism.

A word is necessary here about the *back door* approach of arriving at a philosophy of happiness. Were this chapter to start out with a proposition like "God is the source of all our happiness," this would be met with two things. First the indifference of familiarity and then followed by the unbelief created by my current circumstances. In other words it's easy to say "God is the source of my happiness, but that doesn't square with the circumstances that I am facing." On the other hand, when we realize that the frustration and failure we experience to achieve happiness by looking at this as a practical and very real human problem, as we see the road blocks we realize that we indeed are the problem. We then are open to the remedy as a solution to a great problem, and not simply a proposition of Christian Dogma. Furthermore, we see the solution as a necessary remedy, because I have discovered that I myself am indeed afflicted by those things which have driven the presence of God from me thus effectively cutting off for myself the life of happiness that God wishes to lead me into.

Often times we can view a truth in a new light by studying its antithesis. In so doing we understand the interrelationships of actions and behaviors. Our purpose is not to go from the positive command to love, to the negative command to demonstrate self denial; not to go from the positive command to love the Lord with all one's heart, to the negative command to hate evil, but in examining both we understand more fully what is entailed and where we run amuck. I hope this approach, as well as the concepts, will be helpful in assisting the reader to analyze the culture of the soul as it pertains to happiness and that you will conclude that in him we live and move and have our being and that whatever hinders his presence in your life can be more readily forsaken for that which is life indeed.

May God confirm his special presence in your life as you seek to implement some of the ideas contained in this chapter. May his still small voice be loud and clear to you as you walk with Him.

Marriage Chapter Three

Let us begin our thoughts on marriage with a bold statement of the obvious. Marriage was intended for pleasure! Wow what a cool thing! God our Father and Creator made a special created being, woman, to be our friend, companion and helper. A partner to share our lives with and the innermost thoughts of our being. Someone who will love us unconditionally and we can be ourselves completely and totally. We get to share closeness, romance, and all the joys of physical intimacy and togetherness. Then if the father so wills we are allowed to have children. They are a blast! They share our physical features. They share our temperaments. They are cute and funny (at first; then they get expensive). We raise them together and find joy and fulfillment all of our days... right? And they all lived happily ever after, right? Well not exactly.

Why is it that such a source of joy and fulfillment can be the single greatest source of human pain, turmoil and tension, this side of heaven? In America we have nearly a 50% divorce rate. We have in fact created a culture where people are afraid to get married because they already know it will end in divorce. Many people have been married numerous times and have had their hearts broken and their lives torn apart each time and they are resolved "never again."

I was with a guy recently and upon introduction I told him I was from Minnesota. He seemed proud to inform me that he wasted five years with a girl from Minnesota once. I thought, "How crass." Imagine a perspective of "wasting" five years of one's life with another human being and then throwing them away like a Popsicle wrapper. His tone was one of anger and disgust. How sad.

This is not a new phenomenon. Notice Ecclesiastes 9:9, "Live joyfully with the wife whom thou lovest all the days of the life of thy vanity, which he hath given thee under the sun, all the days of thy vanity: for that is thy portion in this life, and in thy labour which thou takest under the sun" (KJV). In other words, enjoy your wife all your days; it's the greatest gift of all and everything else is vanity in comparison. What a lofty view of marriage. Notice also…

"The contentions of a wife are a constant dripping" (Proverbs 19:13b, NAS). The writer warned about a nagging wife being like a dripping faucet. So too, we can see that the Bible recognizes both sides of marriage, the blessings and the curses, the good and the bad, not unlike today. Like the old saying, "when it's good it's good, but when it's bad it's really bad."

One can hardly listen to any radio and not hear a song about the pain of loneliness, separation, and divorce. Why is there so much failure in the realm of this most basic human relationship? Perhaps your married life has been a disaster and after two or three difficult and heartbreaking relationships you are struggling with some measure of blessing and fulfillment. Maybe your marriage is like my golf game, just when I think I got it together another part of it goes out. Correcting my hook turns a week later into a wicked slice and just when they start to land in the middle of the fairway, my putting game goes south (not that I golf much, but it's true nonetheless).

I have three simple yet profound truths that can revolutionize our world and our own marriages if we choose to let them. Perhaps one of them will encourage you. Don't let their simplicity or familiarity deter you from taking a close look with new eyes.

MARRIAGE IS GOD'S IDEA.

That's right. He created marriage and set some principles in place. Once again we must start with the obvious.

Marriage is one man and one woman, together for life. That's his plan and his way of happiness.

I suppose I need to address homosexuality and lesbianism since it is becoming so prevalent today. Suffice it to say that these are relatively new terms and until recent years there was only one term for both behaviors, namely, sodomy. Perhaps we know the story of the Sodomites whom God destroyed because of their sodomy and perhaps we also know that up until recently it was not only taboo in every culture but also illegal in the United States. So it goes with out saying that anything other than one man and one woman will bring devastation to anyone fooling around with anything different.

Marriage is one man and one woman together for life. This was and is God's design. Separation and divorce is not the answer to your problems. One of the philosophers is quoted saying "we have seen the enemy…and it is us." The only problem with divorce is that when we go our separate ways, we take at least three fourths of the problem with us. I say three fourths, because we take our own half and then we get stuck with half of the baggage from the departed spouse. So contrary to popular thought, divorce is not the answer.

What if I've already been divorced? Are their circumstances where divorce is merited? It's not within the scope of this book to deal with these issues but I will give it some treatment within this chapter.

OUR MATE IS A GIFT FROM THE LORD.

Say that right now …out loud. "My mate is a gift from the Lord." You need to start believing that because it's true! Notice what Proverbs 18:22 says, "He who finds a wife finds a good thing, and obtains favor from the LORD" (NAS). Do you see that! If you have obtained a wife, it's a good thing and you are blessed of the Lord. Do you know how may people are going through life alone, single, and widowed and are yearning for someone to share their lives with? Many. So the statement of faith here is that this is a good thing. This wife of mine (this spouse of mine for the ladies reading) is a *good* thing. It may not seem it to you at times, but let's begin in faith believing God's Word.

Here's another insightful Scripture. "House and wealth are an inheritance from fathers, but a prudent wife is from the LORD" (Proverbs 19:14). Dad can give a monetary inheritance, but a prudent wife is from the Lord. She is a gift from him, just like Eve, created especially for you. I'll let you decide if your wife is prudent and I'm sure she is because 99% of all women clip coupons. That one fact alone makes them prudent. Further evidence of their prudence is their immediate recognition of a very special four letter word: SALE. That's right; I bet your wife is great at sniffing out a bargain. Furthermore, they married you didn't they? If you are questioning their prudence you must also be making a statement about what you're really made of.

Lastly, let's just say when you got married everything was all wrong. You were both unbelievers and really got off on the wrong foot. Well I got news for you in this next concept.

SHE HAS JUST BECOME MRS. RIGHT.

Here's how it works. Romans 2:28, 29 tells us that we *know* that all things work together for them that love God, to them that are the called according to His purpose. So let's suppose that when you got married you were not walking with God. You married the "wrong" person and now you're stuck for life with someone who is totally incompatible. (Purely hypothetical of course, not that anyone would ever think that way.)

According to this verse, didn't God know who you were going to marry? Don't you love him now? Are you not the person described here in this verse? Then the faith conclusion is that she has just become Mrs. Right because God is causing all things, even the decisions you made ten years ago, to work together in your life for good today. Mrs. Wrong just became Mrs. Right. And you Mr. Wrong have just become Mr. Right.

Let's face some sobering facts folks. Suppose you marry the absolute Mrs. Right, even with the perfect mother-in-law. How long will she be that Mrs. Right? About three weeks. Then we discover she is human and has faults, and even the things we admired about her can drive us crazy…and become a constant dripping.

Let me give you a practical real-life example. One of the things that drew me to Judy was her unending smile. She so totally focused on what you were saying, just smiling and nodding and taking in every word. I thought she is the most thoughtful and loving person in the world. To think someone would be that interested in me and smile as she listened. Wow! Two years later I am ready to strangle her because when she is talking on the phone smiling and nodding and I ask her who she's talking to, or please pass the salt, I might as well be talking to the salt shaker itself, because she has not even heard me. In fact she doesn't even know I'm home from work yet!

So with the potential of these types of dynamics taking place, even the best seemingly grounded couples can be on the ropes in no time at all.

I want to share personally how this played out for Judy and me. We were not raised in Christian homes, quite the contrary. We had little to no knowledge of God and His ways and had in fact seeds of destruction in our lives by building our marriage on an improper foundation, because we simply had none. It wasn't long before she was feeling unloved, unwanted, unappreciated, and wanting to leave. Children came fast and furious and this only added to the frustrations. Like most of us we began by meshing two dysfunctional lives together and then tried to unscramble everything from what to do on holidays to how to spend our money. This was a formula for disaster and I can say that I can totally relate, first hand, to the problems most couples face. Were it not for the Lord, His Word, and His people, we probably wouldn't have made it. But some neat things happened over the years as God worked in our hearts. I want to share some of those with you.

As we began to yield ourselves to the Lord we began to grow together in Christ's likeness. We also began to like each other more and more. We even have continued "falling in love" again once or twice through the years. How does that work? It's sounds corny but it's kind of like in the movies. I'll see her sitting there and maybe she's sleeping or reading a book, and the sun is on her hair and her legs are propped up in a simple but sexy way and I think to myself, "Wow, that's my woman! She is beautiful and I get to be married to her!" Or maybe its coming out of a decision making process where she was not too hot on some idea that I had and in her little way she in essence says, " Well, you can do what you want because you're the captain of our little ship, but I don't think it's the right thing to do." And after stewing about it for a few days, circumstances reveal, "She was right! How did she know that?"

Falling in love again is spur-of-the-moment, a dawning realization of how much I truly do love, admire, respect, and appreciate my spouse. It's an awesome thing to experience and to have reciprocated. The truth of the matter is that I actually love Judy far more now than when I married her. We have grown together and have learned to understand each other and truly appreciate our uniquenesses, but it hasn't always been easy.

This leads us to the second important concept, now that we have Mrs. Right, we must realize that...

- **I don't have to change her, I can just enjoy her.**

I have to admit I spent the first five years of our marriage trying to change my wife. I tried to re-parent her. I guess I figured her dad and mom didn't do a good enough job so I was going to pick up where they left off. One little thing I would do that was extremely hurtful is that I would correct her English—in public—frequently. When out with friends we would be bantering back and forth in lively discussion and she would get a little loud and excited (she's Hungarian and Italian mind you) and I would scold her, "Will you let someone else talk?" "Let the guy finish his sentence." "Learn to listen more." "Why in the world did you say such and such?" There were times after a time of visiting with friends I had her in tears. She felt awful and felt she was ruining my life with her incorrect grammar and embarrassing me in public. She would promise never to talk again in public the next time we went out. Then after a social engagement she would say, "Did I say anything to embarrass you?"

Now I wasn't *trying* to be a jerk, I was just one by nature. And of course I had it all rationalized in my head that when she stops crying she will realize that I was right and will thank me for it later. The problem is that she only withdrew more and more and by the time we had been married five years I had her brainwashed by my constant little comments and reminders that she was some type of illiterate with a speech impediment. Being the brilliant Neanderthal type that I am I couldn't figure out where all this inferiority was coming from. I would remind her that she got As in school and I only got Cs. When I reminded her that she took Calculus and I barely made it through Algebra I, it was all to no avail. As a young girl in her mid 20s she became so self conscious that I came to the serious realization that I was well on my way to destroying the beautiful person that God had created her to be.

So I grasped this principle. I stopped trying to change her and I actually started changing me. I realized that she is who she is and I don't have the right, *or the ability,* to change her. I can enjoy her, go with the flow, and watch and see what happens.

Well wouldn't you know it she made it through every social situation without any commentary from me and continues to do quite well. Just making the conscious decision not to try to change her was liberating for both of us. First I could enjoy my wife and really appreciate her. And after numerous social events she felt comfortable exchanging freely again without hyper-analyzing everything she said. I began to see that people really liked her and enjoyed her quite the same way I did when I first met her.

This is a very liberating principle in that we are all very different and we need to let each other be different and not see those differences as a project I need to change, but as something I can actually learn to enjoy. That is indeed out next important life-giving principle

- **Our differences can become a source of beauty and not intolerable tensions.**

They say opposites attract and it is, of course, true. This can be a source of blessing as we learn to work together and allow our differences to compliment one another. However, when we are immature or carnal it is these differences that are sources of irritation and great conflict in marriage.

Judy and I are very different. Opposites, you might say, in many ways. It always amazes me that we can get along so well most of the time in spite of these differences, which are many. Let me outline some of these differences and how they have played out in our marriage. Perhaps you will see yourself in some of this and even find hope for your individual challenges.

One way that we are very different is that she is an incredible people person and I am a project person, a 'type A' personality, and a very goal oriented person. This can be a source of great conflict. Judy enjoys visiting with people after church or after the event has ended, and I am usually in a hurry to get on to the next thing. This usually means I am waiting for her and feeling frustrated because I am not getting to the items on my 'to do' list. This became a source of real tension in our marriage. Spontaneous "visits" would pop up everywhere just in time to ruin a quick trip into Target to pick up two items. Here's how it went.

We would run into Sally Smith, who she hadn't seen in six months; they would begin catching up on all the latest news and rekindling their friendship and sharing stories of our past summer vacation or the kids' Friday night recital. After ten minutes I would take the hint that they were just getting started and wander down to the sporting goods or automotive to give the ladies time to be alone. I would then wander back to pick up our purchases from Judy who, never missing eye contact, would hand them off to me, barely conscious of my presence, and when I told her I would meet her in the car I was not really certain if she even heard me. Ten minutes later she would emerge and ask if I could come back in and look at such and such that was on her list. By this time I am furious and thinking "How can she do this to me?" "It's Saturday and my only day to get something done around the house and she 'wastes' an hour and fifteen minutes on an already too long trip to town." What ensues is where the fireworks begin.

She comes out bubbling over having just had this wonderful serendipitous 'Divine appointment' and is bubbling over with excitement. I on the other hand am usually bubbling over with something else, more like steaming out with wrath and fury. A major collision is about to ensue. Before she can even get out a word, I would usually greet her with some stupid remark about how selfish she was and how next time I was going to run to town alone. Well you've got to know that this is like throwing water on a hot fire and what you end up with is a lot of steam and the result is dead coals. Her thought process, if not her words, was something like this. "You are so selfish. You don't care about me. You know what?... I don't even want to come to town with you anymore, ever! Go by yourself!" Part of her just died inside as I squelched the person she was and the things God was doing in her heart and in her relationships. (I told you I was nearly Neanderthal, although my knuckles don't quite drag the ground when I walk).

This basic personality difference was a significant source of tension while I was fighting it and trying to change it. It wasn't until I started to go with the flow and accept it that I began to change me and truly began to appreciate and enjoy the fruit of her personality.

Let me illustrate. I enjoy going to the ocean. I grew up on the east coast and went every summer. One of the dangerous aspects of the ocean is a rip tide; a fast moving current that is going away from shore because of underwater sand bars and such. When caught in a rip tide, one begins moving away from shore quickly; faster than you can swim! Judy and I actually got caught in one off the coast of North Carolina and we were in the process of being carried out to sea. This is very scary as you see the shore moving faster and faster away from you. So what do you do? You start swimming like crazy, against the current in hopes of getting to shore. You fight it with all your might. After about two minutes you've hyperventilated and burned up all your caloric energy, engaged all the adrenaline in your body and in a word, panicked. Not the right choice of action. But in marriage, this is exactly what we do and in this case, exactly what I did.

Early in our marriage I saw these differences and figured I needed to fight hard to change them before they became habits and patterns (they were actually worse than that, they were personality traits), and tried to furiously change them, but like the rip tide, with all my strength I could not overcome the flow and out to sea I went. So what should one do in a rip tide?

First, don't panic and lose your composure. One can float for a long time in buoyant salt water. The tide is like a stream or river flowing away from shore. The answer then is to swim gently, parallel to the shore until one is out of the current and can then swim back in. This may take some time so it is important not to panic and use up all one's energy. Soon one will be back on dry ground. So it is with these differences in our marriages.

After my resolve not to try to change her (swim against the tide), I began to look for ways that this could be a blessing as I went with the flow. God is so good because here's what comes out of this thinking. Whenever I go anywhere with Judy I always bring a book to read. It's great because I can catch up on some long overdue reading. It gets better. I realize that God using her and the blessings of these visits flow over to me and it is now "our" divine appointment. I realize that if it were not for her, we would have no social life so I am grateful for all the friends she has made and maintained over the years.

Often times she'll remind me about details and goings on of family members, friends of ours who've had a child and what the baby's name is, someone who had surgery, all kinds of life stuff that is important. "How did you know that?" I ask. Didn't you remember when we were visiting with Keri after Bible study?" No, I didn't, because although I was listening, I wasn't' making mental notes. She was because she is an incredible people person and she keys in on these kinds of details. We're on different tracks and she gets a lot of stuff that I don't. This works both ways. My mother calls and we talk for an hour. Ten minutes later I am working on the computer and she says "What did your mom have to say honey?" to which I reply, "Nothin' much." Three weeks later my mom calls again and talks to Judy and she says, "Didn't Paul tell you I had cataract surgery on the 10th?" "No he didn't." Well, it seemed like no big deal to me. She said it was painless, she was in and out in thee hours and the next day she was fine. Sorry, Honey!

So this has become a source of great blessing as together we compliment each other. I love watching her face, the sparkle in her eyes, and that incessant smile when she is conversing with someone with such love and genuine concern and focus. You see, my perspective has truly changed and where there was once tension and anger there is now true love and appreciation. This is wonderful because I have come to realize how much I need her in my life. I can appreciate her and thank God for her. I can also thank God for the ten pages I was able to read while sitting in the car while she was making her list and checking it twice. Now she feels loved, cherished, appreciated, and needed as she is fulfilling vital needs in my life. She keeps me informed about the needs of people around me, reminds me of important dates and events, makes holidays special and often gives me a completely different perspective on how people around me may be thinking that I am totally unaware of. I am grateful for her insights.

In all fairness we have had to work at it, and still do. I warn her when I am going to town that I want to be back at a certain time so if you want to come, let's shoot for that goal. I still bring my book and am open to divine appointments even if that means "Oh honey can we stop over such and such because this is the only time we'll be together in town to do this before thus and so." So I realize that this is something that (although not on my list) needs to be done and I am grateful for the fact that she remembered before we missed the opportunity.

So life is good. I am married to the most perfect person in the world for me, Mrs. Right, and I realize that I don't have to change her, and best of all and I am growing in love and in "like" while appreciating her as a person. Now comes the hard part as we look at the third principle in marriage.

- **Joy in marriage comes in living a life to please your spouse.**

Many years ago I was sitting around the campfire with a bunch of guys who knew me well. They were unsaved – they hadn't made faith commitments at this point in their spiritual journeys. We got to talking about our wives and somehow someone made the statement "It's not my job to make my wife happy. I can't do that." The other guys immediately agreed and it was a settled conclusion. Well I couldn't really let that one fly. Since I'm never one to be controversial (pun intended) I had to disagree so I said something to the effect, "I don't really see it that way guys. I think it is our job to make our wives happy." This was met first with silence and the silence was broken with a crude statement, "That's alright Paul, we all know you're pussy-whipped" (if you'll pardon the vernacular) to which they all burst out in laughter. I mention this because as guys, more so than girls, we really don't get it. It IS our job to make our wives happy. As I reflected on it I was glad at their spontaneous conclusion because they all recognized that at least my behavior demonstrated that I live a life of trying to please my wife.

As I've reflected on this over the years I remembered the traditional wedding vows. It seems to me I remember something about "Will you live with your wife to give her happiness all of your days?" to which we ALL responded "I will" or "I do"! This really comes down to the crux of the matter—if I am doing something that is hindering the happiness of my spouse, I need to fix it. Now I realize that due to the influences outlined in Chapter 1 on Happiness, one's spouse may have issues all their own, and I agree that we cannot *make* someone a happy person, but I am saying it must be our desire and practice. I have a theory that's pretty tried, true, and biblical.

A woman is a mirror. What she is, is a reflection of the input given to her from her husband. You show me a woman who is happy, sane, well-adjusted, poised, responsible, not manipulative, giving, caring, sharing, balanced, and secure, and I'll show you a guy who's tending to the garden of his wife's soul. She's going to mirror whatever we show her. When she looks in the mirror, she sees what we show her. On the contrary, you show me a woman who is immodest, insecure, manipulative, out of control, overspending, and unstable, and I'll show you a guy who is not doing his homework and is probably sowing seeds of doubt, shame, neglect, and insecurity into the soul of his wife. Although it's just a theory, a little word picture of looking at this husband and wife dynamic, it does have biblical foundations from Ephesians 5.

In chapter five we are told to cleanse our wives with the washing of the word and to remove every spot and wrinkle. We are told to nourish and cherish our wives as our own bodies. Paul even goes on to say "for no one ever hated his own body but nourishes and cherishes it," so we too must nourish and cherish our wives and the culture of their souls. You think Paul made it clear enough? Hey guys, you wouldn't smack your thumb intentionally with a hammer because, duh… it's gonna hurt. We all can relate to that. So don't go on hurting your wife, in any way. We've got to learn this nourishing and cherishing stuff, in a word, living to please our wives.

These words somehow seem so feminine, don't they? Nourish and cherish—sounds like breast-feeding to me. Well, let me put it in terms you can understand.

You pick the topic, but you and your wife have a major blow out. The result after the yelling and tears is known as the cold shoulder. It includes, but is not limited to, the following:

- The cold shoulder. Defined as facing the wall with a very clear don't touch me message.
- The silent treatment, which for the purpose of survival is limited to guttural noises and yes and no responses.
- No eye contact. There are two purposes for this. One is because she's too disgusted to look at you and the other is it could eventually soften her resolve to inflict as much pain as possible. You hope it's the latter.
- Offers to write newspaper ads for maid service because things like laundry and meals will now be ancient history.
- The couch all to yourself, until further notice.
- Forget about sex, it's out of the picture; celibate forever doesn't sound fun.

Do I have your attention yet? Sound familiar? What's her point in all this? Half of it is self preservation, but the other half is inflicting as much pain as possible by depriving you of all the rights and joys of your relationship from companionship to intimacy. Chances are this last one really has you concerned. (It's a dirty trick guys, but effective none the less.) Well, how shall we describe this relationship? The perfect word is cold. We might even call it a Cold War.

The cold war is an interesting phenomenon. Remember the United States did it with the former Soviet Union for nearly half a century. We are not trying to destroy each other in open war; we are just trying to co-exist while inflicting pain by withholding goods and services. It's a game of strategy. You know you are in a cold war when you develop an opponent mentality. Then you begin to watch each other with suspicion and distrust. You question each other's motives, ask probing questions and doubt the answers. You look for ways to inflict pain. As the war continues you begin self preservation techniques including establishing a war chest, looking for dirt, squirreling away resources, and as time goes on, considering options. The cold war is not fun. Let's get back to Ephesians.

The word *cherish* actually means to heat up, to soften by heat, and to keep warm! Wow! Now that takes on a whole new meaning in the dynamics of my relationship in the context of the cold war, at whatever stage it has developed. The command is to warm her up and keep her that way.

It's interesting the language we use. I was talking to a 7-year-old boy recently and he said about some girl, "She's hot." "Where did he come up with that?" I thought. We all understand this—*hot* means passionate, sexy, and ready for love. How does the relationship that started out HOT get COLD so fast and stay there? We've got to go from cold, to cool, to tepid, to lukewarm, to warm, and back to hot. Hot is good in the context of marriage.

A few years ago my wife and I took an exotic vacation to a nearly deserted island after 20 years of marriage and 11 children. It was truly like a honeymoon all over again. Why did we wait 20 years to do this? Maybe it had something to do with being broke and raising 11 kids. I cannot describe to you the joy we experienced then and subsequently realizing that we both have the "hots" for each other. What a wonderful feeling to be young, healthy, in love, and enjoying each other. I wish this for everyone.

But what did it take and what will it take in each of our relationships? It takes a thermometer. We have to continually check the temperature of the water. Warm it up and keep it warm. As soon as it starts to cool it should be a warning to us that something is going wrong. Make the correction. I could give a hundred lists and examples, but you know what it takes to warm her up. This is a great way of monitoring our relationship by asking ourselves, what is the temperature of the water? It's amazing what a few degrees will do.

We live in Northern Minnesota and I work construction. Winters can reach 50 degrees below zero, and 30 degrees below for three weeks at a time is not unusual. Last year we purchased a hot tub to put outside on the porch. As I get older, and colder, it's great to come home after a hard day's work and hit the hot tub to unwind, warm up, and work some of those aches and pains. Never having owned a hot tub, I really didn't know a thing about them. I learned that the maximum temperature on most of these tubs is 104 degrees. I am basically a hot person so 104 is really too much for me. I can only stand it for about 5-7 minutes. However 102 degrees is a world of difference. I can stay in for 30 minutes to an hour. One wouldn't think that two degrees would make such a big difference but it does. So now our family has become experts in determining hot tub temperatures. When we go to hot tubs occasionally at the YMCA or a hotel, we guess what the temperature is and see who comes closest. Every time we get in it becomes a game to see who can guess the temperature. I can usually hit it right on the head; it's amazing how sensitive our bodies are.

If I could push this little analogy a little further. Watching the temperature on the hot tub is critical for me because if there is a problem with the heater, or the motor, or the breaker went out for some reason, at 20-30 degrees below zero I could have a small pond in there and a big bill awaiting me. So I keep my eye on it and if I don't go in for a few days or am out of town I'll ask the kids, "what's the temperature?" If there is a problem I need to know right away because I have limited time to get in a part or get it fixed. So, too, with our marriages. The sooner we detect problems, the more time we have to work on them and keep them from causing irreparable damage that is more costly than money.

Hopefully this little analogy will help us in practical ways to always monitor the temperature of our relationship. We can make it a personal game and become experts in detecting when little offenses have crept in and started cooling the waters. Maybe like America and the USSR, the cold wars will become a phenomena of history.

In review:
1. Marriage is God's idea.
2. My spouse is a gift from the Lord.
3. He or she *is* Mr. or Mrs. Right.
    - I don't have to change her, I can just enjoy her.
    - Our differences can become a source of beauty.
    - True joy in marriage comes from trying to please our spouse.

Take a moment and jot down your thoughts. What are you taking away from this chapter? What have you seen more clearly? What steps of action are needed? How is God speaking to you?

May God bless you and may your marriage become a source of incredible joy as the presence of Jesus brings fulfillment through insights and the power to change perspectives and behaviors for that to be a daily reality.

Children Chapter Four

Now as we begin this chapter I hope you realize that you will be stretched on this one. Remember the title of the book, *Thinking Outside the Box*. That means we are going to approach things by setting aside our stereotypes and the preconceived ideas we have and try to look at a subject from a new vantage point.

This chapter has two themes I would like to develop. The first is that children are a blessing from God. The second is that children open the door to many of God's other blessings. So hold on to your hat because here we go.

CHILDREN ARE A BLESSING FROM GOD

Well, this is really no new revelation. Nearly everyone will agree with that. As a culture we've even adopted the language that reflects that. "What a little blessing"; "Is that your little blessing?" It's not unusual to see T-shirts and baby cards to that effect. We realize this intellectually, but how does it play out in our lives? Let's think for a moment of what a blessing is.

The word blessing in the Hebrew language is *asher*. It means happy. Perhaps you remember one of the sons of Jacob was named Asher. Children are a source of happiness. We all recognize this. When someone informs us that they are expecting we say, "I am so happy for you, congratulations!" What joy that child brings when the baby comes. Entire church services stop as the baby's name is announced. The weight and length is declared and there is this strange sense of awe in the whole room as everyone smiles and nods. How about those baby dedications? The parents come all dressed up and the babies are all decked out with little bands and bows on their heads. The place is alive with excitement and happiness. Why? All over a baby! This *is* exciting. It's a happy time.

Remember when the baby was born. We didn't care what time it was. Three a.m. No problem, call everyone. People are delighted when they get a call at 3 a.m. from an excited father. Why? Because they are invited to share in the happiness and no doubt one of the first to be informed. Then, for the next 12 hours phone calls are flying around the planet as everyone remotely close is sharing the joy of this happy event. Yes, it is a universal fact that children are a blessing.

It always amazes me to see advertisers using babies. Now keep in mind that advertisers do nothing without making money or generating sales. Why do they use babies? Because people are fascinated by babies. They are interested in them and they love to look at them. Notice, too, babies unite people. Two moms at the park will start talking spontaneously as they watch their children play. Complete strangers will whip out their wallets and start flashing pictures of their kids at dinner parties, or on vacation. I could walk up to a total stranger on the street and say, "Do you want to see a picture of my kids?" and unless they are in a hurry to go somewhere they're gonna say, "Sure." Even if they're not interested, they are not going to say, "No way pal, I don't wanna see your brats."

The latest trend in showing off the kids is the sports buttons. How proudly we wear them. I think they are awesome. You can wear your kid on your chest in their baseball or soccer uniform right out there for everyone to see. The cashiers in the supermarket lines, complete strangers, will look and ask questions and start telling you about their kids or grandkids. Children are a blessing; we all agree with that. It's got to be universal.

Since we understand this principle, that children are a blessing, I would like to develop two ideas that reinforce this concept. The first has to do with our thought process, namely our attitude towards children and the second has to do with our actions. Let's begin with our thoughts.

SINCE CHILDREN ARE A BLESSING WE NEED TO BEGIN TO VIEW THEM AS SUCH.

If we truly believe children are a blessing from God, Asher, something that makes us happy, and leads us into a state of blessedness, why is there still so much negativity about having children?

First there is the resistance to have children. When young people today get married it's almost a given that they will be on birth control. "We're going to wait a few years before we have children," is a common thing I hear when talking to newlyweds. They start out their honeymoon with sophisticated means of preventing these blessings. *Do we really believe children are a blessing?*

This attitude toward children is not confined to the pews of our local churches. I would guess that a vast majority of evangelical pastors would advocate birth control for young couples and would counsel them through the pros and cons and would at least make sure they discussed their "blessing prevention plan" so at the critical moment everyone knows what to do. *Do we really believe children are a blessing from the Lord?*

Let's talk about abortion. Most people reading this book are evangelical believers and are against abortion. Abortion is the *world's* solution to unwanted children. Why does the world not want children? Because in their heart of hearts they really don't believe children are a blessing from God. Conversely, you see, birth control is the *church's* solution to unwanted children because they too really don't believe children are a blessing from God. The way I see it folks, there is really no difference. Both groups don't want children. Both groups have the same attitude towards children; *it's just the lengths they are willing to go to prevent them that's different. That's the only thing.*

If nothing else, this chapter is a bold call to the church to repent of its ungodly attitude toward children. But the church just doesn't see it that way. Perhaps an illustration will help.

Some years ago I was candidating at a local church and it was just after Right-to-Life Sunday. Wanting to get to know the candidate, the young elder asked me what I was doing to be involved in the right-to-life fight to save the unborn. He went on to inform me that he had just participated in a march of sorts with holding hands across town etc. and wanted to know what kinds of things I was doing. I admitted that I never did a sit-in or picketed, or even worked a booth at a fair. But when history looks back on this period where millions of babies were being killed I'm going to be able to tell my children that I was *having* children.

Anyone can hold a sign and say "children are a blessing," but it takes a real believer to toss the birth control and say, yes, children are a blessing, Lord bless me. While this guy's youngest must be by now in high school, we just had our 12th child a few months ago. His demonstration lasted a weekend; mine is going to last for generations.

Please don't misunderstand me, I am not trying to be haughty, negative, or criticize the grace given to a fellow believer, or their efforts in a good cause, *but folks we've got to start seeing the incongruity of our thoughts on this account.*

Suppose blessings were in the form of $20 bills. Would we say, "OK Lord, thank you for these two…that's all I want…please don't send any more. *I don't see people inventing ways to prevent dollar bills from rolling into their wallets. Do we really believe children are a blessing from the Lord?*

How about abortion? How many believers have gotten caught up in it and actually murdered their own children because they felt so strongly that these children would ruin their lives. I know many believers who've gone down this road only to reap the consequences of serious regret and incredible turmoil and pain. *When we fail to believe and teach that children are a blessing from the Lord, we cause weaker brothers and sisters to stumble and cross that line during times of panic and confusion. Does the church really believe children are a blessing from the Lord?*

I'm going to tell you our story. We wanted a big family; maybe five children. Today that is a big family. After we had three we began using birth control thinking maybe we wanted to be done. Neither one of us were ever really at peace with the methods at hand. Here's how we thought about these things.

The pill is just too intrusive. It's chemically altering a natural process that God had created and there are reports of side effects, including spontaneous abortions and also future sterility. Then there was the IUD, or intrauterine device. A piece of plastic placed inside a woman and left there to grow a bacteria or virus or something that will kill this baby to be or at least eliminate the little guys trying to swim the distance. Again it didn't seem to make sense to us to start an infection inside to kill something that was a natural process. Of course complications can arise with this also. So that left us the condom. OK it does work, but it destroys intimacy in that one is always needing to be prepared to have one, and actually use it, so in spite of these practical inconveniences, it was the most acceptable means we were comfortable with. Of course there is also the rhythm method. But when all is said and done, there are about three weeks out for the month when intercourse is not possible. We scheduled enough things in life and scheduling sex just doesn't seem like something that belongs on my palm pilot or the family calendar. Sex was meant for pleasure and to be a spontaneous and frequent part of our relationship. Its purpose and vital function in our marriage is not only for intimacy, but also for recreation and stress relief, believe it or not. Furthermore, the Apostle Paul said, "Stop depriving yourselves, except for prayer." See 2 Corinthians 7.) So the rhythm method, although the least intrusive and most natural, was also problematic. So for us, we used condoms for a time but grew uncomfortable with the whole process.

After a time we both felt very convicted about it, but we had three young kids and were struggling financially and had a hundred good reasons not to have any more, including, pressure from family and church. So we finally cracked and decided that we were going to give this decision to the Lord. A few months later we were expecting our fourth and it turned out to be four, five, and six. Needless to say, we were ecstatic. We decided from then on that the Lord was truly trying to get our attention in this area and from now on we would leave the choice to him.

There is one other part of this that is essential to share. During my wife's first three pregnancies I prayed for twins. I really did. I prayed hard. I cried out to God. I just thought it would be cool to have two little ones. They're so special and cute. But each time, no twins. Finally my wife said "Sorry honey, I guess I don't make twins." So we sort of forgot about it and then after agonizing and giving the decision to the Lord, that is leaving the decision to him about when and how many children we were going to have, we conceived. We were shocked and surprised when the midwife came to the house at about five months and heard two heartbeats. Needless to say we were dumbfounded. She recommended an ultrasound.

Since we had just dropped our maternity rider on our insurance policy, I called my friend Peter who just *happened* to run a portable ultrasound business. It was a day I will never forget. David, Susan and Daniel filed into the little exam room, no bigger than 7 x 10 and sat quietly on the floor against the wall. Mom laid on the exam bed and I knelt by her head as the technician performed the sonogram. Not long into the procedure he starts making faces. "Is there something wrong?" I asked. Then he asked me if we were using fertility drugs. I looked at the three kids crammed in the corner, one, three and five years old and said, "I don't think so." Then I asked "Are you saying there are more than two babies in there?" He replied, "I can't say…there are too many arms and legs in here." Sure enough, it was triplets. We just started laughing hysterically. We walked out of that place 10 feet off the ground. Here's how it worked out.

We already had two boys and one girl. Our triplets were born and guess what? Two boys and one girl. In one day we went from three to six children. Our family doubled overnight. As I reflected on this I realized that God had actually answered my prayer for twins, with each previous birth. The answer I thought was "no" was actually a "yes," but in a totally different way.

That's what this book is really all about. It's about God giving us so much more than we ever imagine when we let Him. We almost didn't let him! The triplets have been such a source of blessing not only to us, but to everyone who knows us.

Our church was amazing as they got behind us and they really got a blessing through ministering to us. Having the triplets was opening the door for all the other children that the Lord has since blessed us with. Each one is so unique and special and they have been such a blessing to us and to many others as they have grown and developed. As a family we are a fun family to be around. We are very active and play all kinds of sports, are involved in music, take fun vacations together, and bring joy and hope to people all because we have so many children. They are a blessing. That's our personal testimony that children are a blessing from the Lord.

What am I saying? Children are a blessing from the Lord, and we need to view them as such. Let's look at the next theme.

Once we realize that children are a blessing from the Lord, really something that is to be desired, then we need to receive children from the Lord. This requires a change in our behavior – namely surrendering to his Lordship and control of this area of our lives. WE cannot say that "sure, children are a blessing, but I don't want any." It's incongruous.

I am a firm believer that God will never give us more than we can handle in anything, from sickness to money, to children. It's no different. Either he is God, or he isn't.

I'm not going to get into all the details of all the medical conditions that have been served up on the church and the American people by the doctors over the past 30 years to prevent women from having more children; it's not within the scope of this book. Suffice it to say that we've had six children after the botched c-section from the triplets and in spite of my wife's so called "incompetent" cervix, she has succeeded by God's grace to have six children and eight pregnancies.

++++++

CHILDREN OPEN THE DOOR TO GOD'S OTHER BLESSINGS.

In the remainder of this section I would like to bring to your attention an exciting concept—that children actually open the door to God's other blessings. I believe that when we come to him in childlike faith and entrust this sacred and awesome area of our lives into his hands he is delighted to meet us with His loving kindness and tender mercies that others will never experience. Please follow along as I enumerate seven blessings that come as a result of giving this decision to God.

1. It enforces that we are not our own.

We must come to realize that we live for God and his purposes and for others. We've heard a lot in recent years about humanism. Humanism says man is the measure of all things and he determines his own destiny. He determines what is right and wrong, etc., etc., ad infinitum. Isn't the relinquishing control of our lives a manifestation of the Lordship of our creator over our lives? Is this not an acknowledgment in a very practical and tangible way that we admit that he knows what is best for us in these most important decisions? We defer to him and honor him as our Lord.

Once again, I find it so incongruous that many a pastor can preach eloquently on humanism and not get the connection. In the very next breath they are counseling young married people to decide before they get married how many children they want to have and when, etc. We want to fit our lives into neat little manageable packages.

2. It assists us in removing selfishness and growing in Christ-likeness.

As I laid out in Chapter 1, we are selfish people by nature. Most of our reasons for not having children are selfish. They will ruin our fun; we want to travel; it will interfere with my career, with her career, etc. Having children is work. It forces us to deny ourselves and to live for them. When baby cries, someone has to get up and go. So we learn to serve one another. Also as we have bigger families, the children are less selfish because they also have to share resources, watch out for one another, and generally work more at caring for little ones, preparing meals, doing laundry, and often helping with a family business. They learn that the family good is a higher purpose than the individual good. Couldn't our world use a few people who are a little less selfish? Both parents and the upcoming generations?

3. It causes us to move into marital maturity.

This is somewhat of a flip side of the above. I have a theory or belief and, don't misunderstand me, I am not making any hard fast rules about this, but couples who intentionally defer the having of children do not develop into marital maturity and the natural processes of becoming a family. A lot of it is related to selfishness. Let me see if I can explain it.

When couples intentionally defer the having of children, the focus of their lives becomes their careers, making money, and pleasure. By pleasure I mean going on vacations (exotic ones), having your hair done, having your nails done, going to the gym to work out, going to the tanning salon to get ready for your vacation, undue concern about how I look in my bathing suit and the list could go on and on. The longer this marital state continues, the possibility of having children is greatly diminished as couples develop lifestyles, habits, and patterns that are not conducive to having children. Then when children do come along, they cannot enjoy them as much because they interfere with careers, figures, and time out with the guys, or vacations. Then, somewhere along the line an interesting phenomenon occurs. Some people call it the seven-year-itch, but today I think it occurs in about two years because we don't have the commitment or societal pressure to wait years to become disillusioned with our spouses.

As a result of all the focus on self and personal gain and pleasure, these types of individuals are used to having their needs met rather immediately. Some measure of worldly success, if from nothing else than being Double Income-No Kids, has afforded them the nicest homes and cars and they are still young, mid-20s to 30ish.

This gnawing emptiness sets in. She wants kids, he doesn't. He wants kids, she doesn't. When they do have children, they have just enough to make them miserable. They don't know how to raise them, they spoil them. They try not to let the kids interfere with their lifestyles, so they allow Grandma and Grandpa to watch the kid or kids frequently who also spoil them. They have their own rooms, computers, Nintendo's, and of course have to go to Hawaii with the high school band trip. We can see where the escalation of selfishness and the lack of maturity sets in subtly but before we know it there is a definite social pathology fully entrenched.

4. It lays the foundation for a rich period in later years of life and marriage.

Having many children lays the foundation to be a family patriarch—to enjoy your later years with many grandchildren. Let's face it; old people are lonely! Imagine having 20 to 40 grandkids; 50 to 100 great-grandchildren! That means a lot of opportunities for a great social life. Lots of soccer games to go to and birthday parties to attend. I recently met a man who was 78 years old. I met him while scuba diving in the Caribbean. He retired 16 years ago and has been diving with his son and daughter and their families ever since. Of course the Mrs. was along too, she was only 73 and got certified for deep sea diving when she was 63. On their 50th wedding anniversary they went diving with the whale sharks in the tumultuous serf of the Galapagos Islands. That was only two years ago!

Imagine a host of people called family, living all over the planet, where one could go and reside and visit as the royal guest of honor, the family patriarch. Telling stories of the good old days and insuring that future generations remember who they are and where they came from. I can't wait!

5. It is a playing field of faith and an opportunity to see the Lord do miracles on a regular basis.

Surrendering this vital area to the Lord moves our lives into a completely different dimension. We are now in way over our heads and …there's no turning back. Scary I know, but how else are we going to see miracles unless we actually need one? When we build our lives in neat little compartments and figure it all out, what else are we going to end up with other than boring predictability? True serendipity comes when God moves in your life and does something that only he can do and you and all the kids see it and it's awesome. I could write an entire book on God's miracles and provision alone, but I will be talking about some of these types of things in the chapters on finances and education.

6. It is a means of making money.

That's right, children help you make money. It works in two ways. First of all, you as father and provider and bread winner have a huge responsibility. After all, you brought all these kids into this world and "whose gonna feed and clothe all those kids?" So the rhetoric goes. The answer is you are! With God's help of course. You're going to cry out to God to get you a good job. You and the Mrs. are now praying together for that promotion. Now you are working a second job maybe to make a few extra dollars, say delivering newspapers from 4 to 6 a.m. before you go to your real job, or maybe your wife is.

Perhaps you and the Mrs. are going to squirrel away a few dollars and start your own business. The bottom line is that "poverty is the mother of invention." People with large families are creative and resourceful and put themselves in positions where God can bless them financially.

Once the kids are grown up, say around 10 years old, they can start making money for you. That's right; child labor. It's worked for centuries and still does. More on this in the chapter on finances. Seriously though, many businesses start as family businesses and they are very efficient in profit margins and generating capital.

7. It's fun.

Yes, having a large family—as many children as God sees fit to give you—is really a lot of fun. We have children from one to 23. I can enjoy skiing with several of them, bouncing a happy baby on my knee, playing family games, playing music together, or just horsing around doing chores. We really don't need a whole lot by way of friends. We always have someone around to do things with. We do stuff together as a family. We are our own best friends. We have a blast just being together and laughing at each other and cheering one another on. We go to a music recital or sporting game and then afterwards come home and analyze the game, the plays, and the coaching. In our home we do not have a TV. We have a wood stove. It's great entertainment. We sit around from 7 to midnight some nights just talking and sharing the day's events. As the children get older it becomes so interesting. We discuss everything from what's going on at church or the pastor's Sunday sermon, to solutions to peace in the Middle East. Life is full, overflowing, robust, challenging, entertaining, happy, blessed. Why? Because years ago we changed our attitudes that children are a blessing from the Lord and then we changed our behavior and decided to receive them as such.

Take a moment and ponder this. Take a few! You might want to discuss it as a couple! Seriously though, it is important to determine *what God is saying to you as a couple.* I have shared with you *our* story. The worst thing you can do is say "Look at this wife; look at this husband, here's what you should do." God gives each of us different grace.

I know one couple who ran down this path and there was not harmony and unity. Unfortunately the result was a difficult divorce after years of struggling. It is important to let the Holy Spirit speak to you and give you one step at a time and to keep the dialogue open with Him. Remember this book is about walking with Him. It's not about a bunch of rules that are "formulas to success." These are principles which *when whispered by the Holy Spirit to your spirit* and united by faith can produce abundant life in your experience as they have in ours.

Education of Children
Chapter Five

As we begin this section on education we realize that we have basically three choices before us for the education of our children, namely, public school, private school, or home school. My purpose in this chapter is to share my thoughts and feelings as well as our family's experiences in education. Perhaps, unlike other chapters, I will not be quoting as much scripture and offering somewhat of a "Thus saith the Lord" tone as I tend to do in some of the other chapters. Although I could do more of that, in the interest of brevity and keeping this book a practical book and not an academic or scholarly work I would rather just share experiences and perspectives without citing cross references or verses and let the reader decide if what is written reflects reality, or is a mere *flatis vocus*, a puff of air.

The foundation of my educational ideas flows out of my experiences as a youth. As I've grown and actually gone to college and done some studying on education, educational theory, psychology, and sociology I have largely confirmed the understandings I developed as a youth. Let's jump right in and begin with the basics.

Education is a big waste of time! Should I repeat that for the effect? I said, "Education is a big waste of time!" (Please don't send me letters yet; first finish the chapter and possibly the book.) Seriously though, as a kid I felt that from the fifth grade on, I was totally wasting my time. I hated school. I got "behind" in math and never really learned my times tables, so I hated math. My 3rd or 4th grade teacher made fun of me and that made things worse. I was not a good reader and I don't remember ever actually reading a book until the 8th grade. I felt history was a complete waste of time. Why would anyone want to rehearse what a bunch of dead people did hundreds of years ago? If there was such a thing as ADHD, I would have been the poster child.

There were a few things that interested me in life, sports, BMX racing and jumping, skateboarding, camping and exploring in the woods with my dog Sport, building forts, floating on homemade rafts in the stream after it flooded its banks in the spring, sleeping out under the stars, and from 8 years old on, making money on my daily paper route. I was a typical boy I suppose. For me school was really a waste of time. I was emotionally immature because I really didn't want to learn.

This is the first problem with school (and I am going to use this term "school" interchangeably with the public school or public education.) **It was a waste of time because it was trying to teach someone who didn't want to learn or was not ready to learn.** Furthermore, because of its cookie cutter approach, everyone had to learn the same things at certain ages. If you didn't fit the schedule, you were behind or advanced or whatever, and if that "whatever" wasn't average or normal, it wasn't good. The bottom line is that it wasn't me. The cookie cutter approach almost killed me. The truth of the matter is that after I became a believer in my young teen years, I became a voracious reader and an independent thinker who loved learning almost anything.

I remember as a kid of 15 years old I used to subscribe to Scientific American, Psychology Today, Newsweek, and used to take home the Dictionary of Philosophy from the school library to read at home. Why? Because I found it all fascinating and I had a desire to learn.

We are wasting our time if we are teaching people who don't want to learn.

THE PROLONGING OF ADOLESCENCE

Education is a waste of time today for the same reason, but also for another very important one. It steals 12 to 25 years of a person's life. We spend 12 years in our foundational education, then 4 years to get a college degree, then another two – four years for a master's degree, then another two to six years for a doctorate. It's not unusual today to still be in school at 30! How many people are going back to school to get second degrees and advanced degrees well into their 30s, 40s and 50s? I need to clarify something here. I am not against education. What I am against is all the monkey business associated with going to school to get a degree. In order to 'matriculate' (who comes up with these terms any way? It sounds like a medical condition) you need 27 hours of electives including 12 credits of PE, (which could include walking or bowling [of course at $300 per credit hour why not offer walking and bowling]) and introduction to drama, and underwater basket weaving. I'm serious folks. School is still a waste of time today as it was for me 30 years ago, only for different reasons.

You take a young person in the prime of their lives and stick them in a classroom from birth to 30, no wonder they can't do anything (and don't want to). No wonder they all want to be computer geeks and have desk jobs! We've kept them in a test tube all their lives, the public school! If you don't think that public school today is a waste of time you are greatly deceived. You have been mass manipulated by society's social engineers and bought the whole shebang, hook, line, and sinker.

Doesn't' it strike you as strange that the kid goes off to school for 7 to 10 hours a day and then has to come home and do HOMEWORK? I could never understand this. Isn't the 8 hour school day enough? Why is it that my kids can learn all this stuff in 2-4 hours a day over a few years?

Think about this. George Washington was the chief land surveyor for the state of Virginia at 17 years old! He was nearly a millionaire by today's standards! Jonathan Edwards entered Yale at 14, I think it was, and he was already accomplished in Greek, Hebrew and Latin! Benjamin Franklin started apprenticing at his uncle's print shop as a boy about 10 and at around 16 years old, I believe it was, he swung a deal with his uncle for an old printing press that wasn't working. Little Bennie tinkered with it literally in the corner of his uncle's shop and soon started a publication called "Common Sense," which effectively made him millions. Ben Franklin essentially retired at 42 and pursued a life of politics, diplomacy, inventing, and just doing whatever he wanted to for himself and for the good of the country.

Compare that to today's educated people. Do you realize that today you need a license and at least a thousand hour course, a degree, and permit from the state department of commerce just to cut hair? *Folks, things have gotten way out of control!* What's worse is that we not only let it happen, but we continue to go along with it! We send our young people to it all their lives! We wouldn't have this country we have if all of our founding fathers were in school for the first 30 years of their lives because they were worried about what people thought about them and so they could have a piece of paper hanging on the wall back in England. They would also be so brainwashed that they would still be sitting around petitioning England for the right do grow their own tobacco!

One of the great purposes of education is exactly that, to waste time. We must keep people in school so we can have a work force, namely a dumbed-down populace that have spent 30 years of people telling them when they can sit, when they can stand, when they can go on vacation, when they can have a sick day, when they can graduate, when they can do anything. This is not education, it's schooling. Beloved, fish live in schools, not people! Doesn't that tell you something? We wonder why we have a peer pressure problem. Go figure! "School" will never, I say again, never, produce independent thinkers and creative geniuses, it cannot. Sure a few may survive school and still have a few brain cells left, but they will not be created there.

The American educational system founded by Dewey and others was taken from the Indian Caste system. This system sought to control the lower castes in order to regulate society. This was discovered through the co-mingling of Americans and citizens working in the British colonies of India in the 17th century. You can read about this in John Taylor Gotto's book titled, *The Underground History of Education in America.* A fascinating read and a must read for anyone thinking critically about education. Incidentally, I stumbled upon this book at a bargain book table at a home schooling fair and in the next 6 months had a life-changing experience as a result of it. Essentially what I have written here and experienced personally in my own educational musings, John Gotto discovered professionally after 35 years of exemplary teaching in the public schools, being awarded teacher of the year for New York City and then doing extensive research on education and the foundations of it in our country. I knew I was right in my heart but it was very reassuring to have someone lay out the reasons why and the historical underpinnings of my ideas, completely independent, of course, of my foregone conclusions.]

The education system that our country was founded on was brilliant in that it fostered true education, creativity, and the entrepreneurial spirit.

I believe this is God's plan and ideal, a learning system that is based on real life and one that doesn't leave people starting their careers at 30 years old and 60 to 160 thousand dollars in debt, paying it back for the whole of their now fledgling married lives. Now that they've graduated from Harvard law school, they *need* a starting salary of $80,000 a year to pay back their loans and what's worse is that they have been told for four years that they are the "social elites" and they *deserve* a starting salary of $80,000 per year (at 29 years old). Many of these people haven't even done anything yet outside of working at entry level jobs, yet they are the ones who will become our politicians and government workers. No wonder our country is in a crisis!

I realize that I am overstating the case and I realize there are many good people in law schools and med schools and engineering schools all over the country, but you've got to, in your heart of hearts, say a hearty amen to these trends that we all see and that are created as a result of our system.

You see, education in America is totally screwed up because it's based on the public school system. Universities were established for learning and for education. Professors were practitioners and the classroom was meant to be life. Read of the great physicians like Walter Reed and John Jay who saw 25-50 patients a day and taught classes. Not so any more. Professors all have to have PhDs today. How do you get a PHD today? By spending 20 years in a classroom, not by doing something with your life! What we need today is radical change. Let me explain.

What children really need is a basic education in reading, writing, and arithmetic. That's it! About four years should give everyone the basics. Then, those who want to go on into a specialty should study that course for a few years including heavy apprenticeships, much like law school and med schools do. I believe children should do more work in their younger years and not attend school with peers as it only breeds foolishness and social pathologies.

Boys between the ages of 12 and 15 should go to the marketplace and work with their fathers, uncles, brothers, or should be guided in starting their own businesses.

What is it going to take? Faith and courage! Most people who read this will not do it because they are really afraid. Afraid of what people will think, and how will my kid make it outside of the system, outside of the box! Afraid to tell your boss that you need to take you kid to work for the next two years. Afraid to find a job that will let you. Unfortunately, too, our society is too far gone to allow this kind of thing.

We have child labor laws, mandatory school attendance laws, and God knows we have the whole insurance problem. Aren't you just sick to death of being told what you can and cannot do because "our insurance companies won't let us"? This is second only to the plethora of attorneys swarming like sharks just waiting to take the case. People can't defecate today without an attorney and an insurance policy! It's sad to see the state that our country has degenerated into.

Well, here's what we did. I'm going to make this real simple. Momma gets the kids reading. Dad helps out occasionally reviewing any concepts mom is working on. This could happen any time. My oldest son David didn't read until he was about 8 and lots of people were rather concerned about this both down at the church and over at grandma's too. Mom gets the kids going on basic math. Dad helps out, teaches a few lessons, and helps through the roadblocks. Then the kids are given freedom to learn on their own.

I tell my kids once they are old enough to read, "I am not going to teach you. If you want to learn you've got to do it on your own. I am not going to fight with you or argue with you, or see you fighting with your mother. If you don't want to do your math, then don't. You are the one who is going to end up stupid not me. You have to live with the educational choices you make. Not me or your mother." And we stop teaching any child that is not wanting to learn or not learning on their own.

We provide an educational environment, not school. We buy books, lots of them. Text books, encyclopedias, dictionaries, historical novels, brain teasers, puzzles and enigmas, nature books, some children's fiction to increase reading speed and comprehension, and we turn them loose. We try to watch what they pick up on, what they like, what they gravitate towards. We encourage writing and grammar as it becomes needed. I read to the kids some when I have time. I do read a lot myself as I go to bed at night, and I discuss things with my kids, so they see that education and reading is a joyful and lifelong process, even Dad does it. He loves it and I do too. The result of this is that education is not compulsory. We do it because we get to and we want to, not because we have to. It's a totally different animal! We now remember things, because we are leisurely engaging the material for enjoyment and pleasure, rather than cramming for the test.

This brings me to tests, grades, and comparison. We usually don't get involved with grading and using national tests for several reasons. 1. Tests test what you teach, not what you know. My kids know a lot about carpentry, electrical, plumbing, cleaning up, adhesives, paints, chemicals, fastening, sales, marketing, horses, sheep, goats, canning, flowers, changing babies, welding, estimating jobs, hiring employees, firing employees, making money and losing money, folding laundry, God and the Bible, church history, but I have yet to see this kind of stuff on tests. So if my kid takes the test, the test has the wrong questions on it and when the results come back it says, "You're stupid, or you're average" when it hasn't touched where or what the child is in relation to our reality. The only bearing is its relationship to the system's reality, which is different from ours.

- **TESTING**

I am not worried about the national norm reference tests. Every kid takes them every year from ages 7 to 16, it's the law. Some of our children are in the 90 to 99 percentile as average. Others are in the 28. I don't worry about it. In fact most years I don't even let the kids see the results. Why? If they are high up, they get a big head and start thinking they are something special. If they are behind they feel bad and start labeling themselves as stupid or slow. We might point out things they should work on i.e. writing mechanics, spelling, etc., but we don't dwell on it. We might look them over with the child for 5-10 minutes, then they get filed and forgotten. I want my kids' self esteem to be base on reality—what they can do—not what some piece of paper tells them they can do, which leads us to the old diploma thing.

- **DIPLOMAS AND GEDS**

What do you do about diplomas and graduation? It cracks me up how people get so worked up over this. And get so serious about it. This is why my system is radical, I know, and I'm not saying you should copy it, but here's how I view that whole thing. A credential is only as valid as the organization who issued it. Since I don't value the public education, why would I want their credential? It has no meaning to me. I don't want the content, so why would I want the culmination? Furthermore, I think everyone in this world knows that a public high school diploma is just about useless today. I feel bad for kids who are adults at 13-14 and have to spend the next four years in school. People can get a diploma and hardly read or write. It doesn't' mean anything! How can it? You can go down and take a GED test after studying for a few weeks. If a kid is playing heads up ball he should be able to walk in and pass a GED test in the 7th or 8th grade. The reason I don't have my kids do that is because, unfortunately, the term GED today means "too dumb to graduate." This really is a shame because being educated should not be measured by how many years you sat in a classroom, but by what you know. If a kid can pass a GED test in the 7th grade, he should be awarded a diploma from his local school district. Isn't it the education that we are after? But because of the system, it's not. We're really after the piece of paper. Who really cares what we know or don't know?

I just tell my kids that they need to say that they graduated from a private school; a very private school. Whoa, kind of elite eh? (You have my permission to graduate your kids from the same school.) What about a diploma. Let me ask you a question. How many times have you had to show your diploma? I never had to. If they need one, I will print one up on the computer and make it real official looking. I haven't needed to yet because what they really want to see is a transcript. Oh yes, the magic transcript. It is your right of passage to higher education. Now what do we do. Let's look at this.

- **TRANSCRIPTS**

When David was about 7 years old I was raking leaves in the yard. Off in the woods not far away was a thicket and in that thicket was a ground hog hole. Every once in a while the ground hog would be seen scurrying across the yard making his way to his home. One day David said, with a tone of determination and tenacity, "I'm gonna catch that guy!" I went on with my raking and later in to prepare some food for the grill. Moments later, while standing at the sink, I heard a voice calling through the window from down below. "Dad, come out here I want to show you something." "What is it son? I'm busy; I can't right now" I said. "Well just look out the window

Dad," was the reply. There he was holding that critter by the tail up over his head for me to see, just as proud as ever. So here I am 12 years later thinking, how in the world am I going to get that on his transcript? They're just not going to get it. Think of the planning it took to catch that thing. Think of the engineering, think of the determination, think of the PE, think of the courage as he recounted to me how he scrambled after that thing across the yard, into the thicket, and as it disappeared down into the hole right in front of him, he dove for the hole, baring his arm to the shoulder just in time to get it by the tail and retrieve it back to daylight. I suppose that's what happens when you tell a 7-year-old boy something so absolutely tempting can't be done!

Back to the transcript. In a nutshell I simply recounted in random rambling order (much like this chapter), everything I'd ever remembered David doing and how proud I was of him and how I was certain that anything David set his mind to do he was smart enough and determined enough to do. Wouldn't you know, that transcript, coupled with an application (and of course a check for admission) got him into college. Funny how all that works.

In all seriousness though, by this time David had quite an impressive resume. He had been working in our family business full time for about five years. No exaggeration. He had built houses from the ground up, literally including all the cement work, sheet rocking, taping, painting, roofing, siding, and trim. That year he had designed, sold, and built two custom homes for clients and managed those homes and several other remodeling projects which netted our family nearly $150,000 in gross. He got his solo pilot permit when he was 16 years old, was an accomplished pianist, played violin in the local symphony, and had a long list of other accomplishments. The point is that he was able to do all this stuff because he wasn't sitting in a classroom from 7 to 17; he was out there doing it.

The transcript issue was a little different for Daniel. He was not going to a small college, but a major university with around 17,000 students. I brought my paperwork to admissions and the counselor asked for the transcript. I gave him the two-page typewritten document. He looked it over and said he would bring it to the admissions officer. He came back two minutes later and said "I'm sorry, we need the transcript. It's a document that looks like this" as he handed me an official transcript with courses, descriptions, and grades. I looked at it and said, "Yes, I understand that this is *a* transcript, but in *our* school *this* is what our transcripts look like. We use an eclectic and non traditional approach. We don't teach classes and we don't grade, so this *is* our transcript," and I handed it back to him. (Sounded pretty official to me as I held my breath to see what he would say.) "Oh", he said, "I will tell the admissions officer." (You've got to love these terms eh? The admissions officer. He's the education police. Again the establishing of authority, making rules, and controlling those who are willing to be under those artificial guidelines.

When we break away from the group, we drift into uncharted waters. There may be awkward situations. It's like a real estate appraisal. They have got to find comps. Comps are homes in the same area that sold for what you are asking to sell your house for, or to borrow against it. But there may not be anything comparable, because your home is totally unique. So it is with children.

At 16 and 17 David was supervising 40-year-old men with 9 years in the union and working circles around them. Our second son Daniel was by his side and had many of the same experiences. It was amazing what those two could accomplish. They literally did more in two days than a five man crew would do in a week. You see, the market place and the dollar drive the education process. Education has to be driven by real world stuff to be effective and the bottom line is that people can't argue with success. I am not sending David to school so he can get a job to make money so he can *be* a success. *He already is a success!* At 20 years old David (or Daniel) could go to work for any company in the country as a construction manager and make $70,000 a year, but why would he want to when he could make twice that working for himself and employing others? We've got to totally change our perspectives and begin thinking outside the box. Well, let's get back to college.

David earned a four year undergraduate degree in a little over one year. He had almost all of his credits completed and he returned to work for the family business and over the next 8 months finished up the remaining classes. So how did he do it?

He did most of it through CLEP and Dante's tests, which he transferred to an accredited regional school specializing in distance learning and graduated from there. He would study the material on Monday and Tuesday and take the test on Wednesday. He would study on Wednesday evening, Thursday, and Friday, and take the next test on Saturday. David averaged 6 credits per week for almost a year, mostly teaching himself the classes—courses like macro and micro economics, , English literature, statistics, business management, college math, algebra II, calculus and trigonometry, physics, and a host of rather rigorous classes. It was really unbelievable. (Calculus did take him three weeks to pass the test.) Why was David able to do this seemingly impossible mission? I believe it was because of the superior education he received by not being formally educated. His mind and head were clear and able to assimilate information in ways that we can't understand because we are so stuck on the old paradigm.

It is a little like Roger Bannister who was the first to run the mile in four minutes thus breaking the mental barrier for hundreds who would do it after. We cannot think outside the box because we've been so programmed to focus on the little square, we're not even aware that there *is* an outside the box, especially when it comes to education. But things are changing.

Educational authorities today are getting more and more used to eccentric students and home schooling. Many universities even have clearly written policies regarding admission of home school students and even transcripts. Schools are actually desirous of students that do have some uniqueness and are not just cookies from the cutter.

- **INTERNET AND COMPUTERS**

I also believe the internet has and is drastically changing the way we view education today. We live today in the information age. Let's face it, how much do we really need to know? I can go on a Google search and type out "statistics on venereal disease in the former Soviet Union for women over 40" and instantly get no less than 10 relevant research papers and scholarly articles. We don't really need to learn that much today (I am talking about at the high school level,) we just need to manage information, and know where to find it. Even the tests at schools today are Open Book. What's up with that? It wasn't that way when I was in school (which wasn't that long ago). Computers aren't even a mystery any more. How many 10 to 13-year-olds do you know who can swap out a hard drive, upgrade memory, download and install programs, set up a network, or post a website? Lots. Information is everywhere and it's not the educated who are going to survive and thrive, it's the fast and the versatile. The ones who can find the information the fastest and keep up with changing trends in whatever field they are in are the ones who are going to go places.

It's a different world and there is the dawning of a new era in education.

- **RESULTS**

I need to highlight some educational results before I move on. As David was burning up 6 credits per week, I had the dean of the school call me one day. I was on a two year payment schedule for a four year degree in what they called the "fast track program." Since David was doing a semester every two weeks, he was effectively three fourths done in seven months and although I was on time with my payments, I was at least a thousand dollars behind if you reckoned by the credit hour. They forbade him from taking any more tests. I explained to the guy that I didn't send my son there to have him sent home or to fail and that regardless of the payment schedule, I wanted him to continue to progress through his studies. I informed him that it would not be for another four weeks before I could get the money. He said "no deal," so that is the reason that David came home. Otherwise he would have finished in three more weeks and graduated within one year. It took him four or five months to get the credits while living at home and traveling 100 miles away to get the tests at the nearest university.

He continued to do well through his first year of law school in which he is currently enrolled. This was his first experience in a traditional classroom with a competitive curve grading system. How would he do? As of the first semester he was in the top 3% of his class. What's amazing about this is that he ran a business during his entire first year, working nights and weekends at times and hiring workers and subcontractors.

We give God the praise and glory for his grace in our lives but also realize the fruit of David "quitting school" when he was 10 and coming to work with Papa, building houses and supervising employees. It works, folks, and the results have been quite serendipitous.

Dare to be bold. Seek the Lord. Are you disturbed at what's going on? This chapter is my invitation for you to think creatively and genuinely "outside the box" when it comes to the education of your children. I trust this chapter has caused you to think, challenged some of your decisions, and I'm sure confirmed others. May Jesus lead you and your family and children entrusted to you into all truth for his Name's sake.

As I have reviewed this section on education I realize that there is little biblical support for that which I've espoused here. I do think it's important that this is not simply a book on my ideas, or what we have done, but what we trust is OF HIM and is therefore supported by the Word of God. I could go into a lot of scriptural support and argumentation for this but let me list a few, by way of broad brush strokes, and let the reader also allow the Holy Spirit to "bear witness with your spirit" concerning the truth of these things.

Mainly, our minds and our children's minds are a gift from God. They are also created by God and are to be used to glorify Him and enjoy Him in all that we do. As such it is imperative that we educate them accordingly. It is a high and holy calling from the Lord because we are to "love Him with all of our heart, soul, *mind*, and strength" (Deuteronomy 6). The proverbs are full of admonitions to seek wisdom and to gain knowledge. Wisdom can be defined as "seeing life from God's perspective." It is understanding His ways in all things, which as we have been seeing is often times counterintuitive to the world's. Who could not come to this conclusion when considering the proposition of evolution? If evolution isn't the absolute stupidest thing I have ever heard I don't know what is. The scientific community accepts that Louis Pasteur proved the whole concept wrong nearly three hundred years ago in his experiments on abiogenesis. He proved that life cannot come from non-life. Yet the whole of evolution is based on this foundational premise. If I were to enumerate the "foolishness" of not only evolution, but of so many of the social concepts and educational theories that have come down through the public education system I would need a wheel barrow to deliver the manuscript.

Let's consider knowledge.

To give subtlety to the simple, to the young man knowledge and discretion. —Proverbs 1:4

The fear of the LORD is the beginning of knowledge: but fools despise wisdom and instruction. —Proverbs 1:7

For that they hated knowledge, and did not choose the fear of the LORD. —Proverbs 1:29

Yea, if thou criest after knowledge, and liftest up thy voice for understanding. —Proverbs 2:3

Then shalt thou understand the fear of the LORD, and find the knowledge of God. —Proverbs 2:5

For the LORD giveth wisdom: out of his mouth cometh knowledge and understanding. —Proverbs 2:6

When wisdom entereth into thine heart and knowledge is pleasant unto thy soul. —Proverbs 2:10

Receive my instruction, and not silver; and knowledge rather than choice gold. —Proverbs 8:10

I wisdom dwell with prudence, and find out knowledge of witty inventions. —Proverbs 8:12 (KJV)

Every prudent man dealeth with knowledge: but a fool layeth open his folly. —Proverbs 13:16

The tongue of the wise useth knowledge aright: but the mouth of fools poureth out foolishness. —Proverbs 15:2

The lips of the wise disperse knowledge: but the heart of the foolish doeth not so. —Proverbs 15:7

The heart of the prudent getteth knowledge; and the ear of the wise seeketh knowledge. —Proverbs 18:15

The eyes of the LORD preserve knowledge, and he overthroweth the words of the transgressor. —Proverbs 22:12

Have not I written to thee excellent things in counsels and knowledge, —Proverbs 22:20

And by knowledge shall the chambers be filled with all precious and pleasant riches. —Proverbs 24:4

What a wealth of insight. First of all, knowledge and wisdom are inseparable from the person of God. If we would know him, if we would fear him, if we would seek him, we will find knowledge. Jesus Christ is indeed the embodiment of all wisdom and knowledge. All the treasures of wisdom and knowledge are found IN HIM! (See Colossians 2:3.) Beloved if we take seriously the command to seek him, then we will become the wisest and most knowledgeable people in the world! It cannot be otherwise. The real question is why do we need the public schools and their diplomas and degrees? Let's consider this.

Is not the purpose of a degree gaining credentials in the eyes of the world? I am not against credentials. Nor am I against credentials in the eyes of the world, because it is in fact, this world in which I have to maintain my existence and before whom I have to give a reason of the hope that is within me to any who ask. What I am against is *what I have to do to get that credential*. I am not going to dishonor God to please the world. I am not going to be spoiled by the philosophies of this present age rather than live according to the glories of the person of Christ. I am not going to become educated in the foolishness of evolution and Freudian lunacy in order to be approved in this world. Neither do I feel particularly kind to the fact of spending money to engage in these activities. No, rather I am going to seek the approval of One. There is a greater credential that I am after and that is pleasing the one who made me and who works all things after the counsel of his will. When we submit ourselves to these human institutions and the societal pressures of higher education, what does it say about who we are really living for? Let's look at another aspect of this.

Scripture tells us to "Number our days that we might present to thee a heart of wisdom" (Psalm 90:12) and to "redeem the time for the days are evil" (Ephesians 5:16). Life is the most precious resource we have. Time is what our lives consist of. Why is it that God's people are so bound up wasting years of their precious lives and that of their children's, not to mention money, to get an education? It is as though the education today has become the end. No, getting out there in the work force and making money and better yet, making a difference is the end. I can remember sitting in class after class of anthropology, geology, sociology, psychology, etc with my blood literally boiling not only listening to such foolishness and wasting my time doing so, but also paying to do it. I vowed I would not subject my children and my heritage to succumbing to such wasteful nonsense. It could possibly be even a little redeeming if there were even room for the slightest dissent from all this foolishness. It was not the case 20 years ago when I went to college and it's only gotten worse. Imagine today God's heritage, our precious youth sitting in classes to learn the appropriateness of sodomy. Not only having their minds twisted up by learning of its appropriateness, but also being brainwashed into thinking that any contrary thoughts are bigotry, insanity, intolerance, and violent hatred. How far must this humanistic experiment go before God's people abandon it for what it is, a bankrupt system hostile towards the things of God.

When we live for the credentials of the world we deny our Lord and Master who says "Thou shalt have NO other Gods before me." When we compromise and trade that which is pure, best, noble, and truth-loving, for that which is popular, accepted, and common place, we deny our Creator's rightful place—as the one for whose approval we are living. When I think of this I can only think of the words of Ephesians 5:6—

Let no man deceive you with vain words: for because of these things cometh the wrath of God upon the children of disobedience.

Everything that the public school and worldly system stands for in its arrogance against God is an object of the wrath of God and a product of the children of disobedience. When believers belly up to the table and eat their fill and say, "Oh it will not affect me; we're here as missionaries," I can only cringe as I wonder if they actually believe these lies or if they are so deceived.

One other passage comes to comes to the forefront as we consider this area of credentials.

The fear of man bringeth a snare: but whoso putteth his trust in the LORD shall be safe.—Proverbs 29:25 (KJV)

There it is folks right there in broad daylight. The need for worldly credentials is right there for all to see. It's based on the fear of man rather than on the fear of God. Submitting ourselves to compromise and worldly ideas, institutions, and paying the Lord's money for these things is evidence that we care more about what man thinks than what God thinks. Notice too, that it "brings a snare." So many of God's people are ensnared in the education trap. Worried and bound by fears. Worried about what people think. Worried about how my kid is doing. Fearful of how my kid is going to make it in this world. WHERE IS YOUR GOD? I have to ask you. This is a trap and a snare and God's people are bound.

Notice that those who trust in the LORD will be safe. If we really trusted in the Lord, we wouldn't worry about all this foolish stuff. Comparing our kids with other kids—it's foolish and unscriptural. If we are trusting in the Lord and seeking him and his wisdom and the knowledge that stores up for us, we should be the most educated people in the world.

If we have true education, we will be useful. If we are useful, we will have jobs. If we are useful and productive, we will have good jobs and will be incredible assets to our employers. I have taught my kids to be employers, and not to look for jobs. They are running businesses while they are in college and are hiring others, not looking for jobs. No, their future is safe because they are trusting in the Lord.

Let me clarify one thing for the reader who is going to write me off and throw the proverbial baby out with the bathwater.

As I've said earlier, this idea of credentials has gotten out of hand in that one even needs a license to cut hair. Credentials are unfortunately not only a good idea in this world, but have also become the law. Be it right or wrong this is the legal development of our country. One cannot practice law without passing the state Legal Bar Exam. To become a physician today one needs a medical degree and to pass a state board exam. I am a contractor and have a license from the state and have also passed an exam. We must also keep in mind that we need to "respect what is right in the sight of all men" (see Romans 12:17) and submit unto the governing authorities (when they are not in violation of the Word of God; see Romans 13:1). By the same token, we also have a right to *demonstrate* what is right in the sight of all men. We can create our own credentials and alternative ways of gaining credentials, which must be accepted by governing authorities since the results are equal or greater than their current systems. It is our responsibility to see to it that they recognize our accomplishments and assign the appropriate credentials where appropriate.

No, there is no glory in ignorance. There is no glory in poverty. Ingnorance, slothfulness, and corresponding poverty are never respected in the sight of all men, but are universally objects of pity. On the other hand, knowledge, diligence, and riches who can argue with?

Thankfully the governmental system of free enterprise under which we live here in the United States is conducive to gaining knowledge through a proliferation of educational materials. It fosters economic success to all who exercise diligence in the market place whether they are self-employed or work for others, and the result is that any person can amass wealth here in America. When we teach our children to be wise and attain knowledge, to be diligent and industrious and attain wealth, then we will have the attention of the world, their respect, and God gets the glory and not some college or university. Let us now turn our attention to this all important topic: money and wealth.

Money Chapter Six

Although I've never quantified it, I am told that Jesus had more to say about money than anything else. I believe it. After all, he was a relevant guy. He was always addressing what was on the minds of the people. And what do we spend most of our waking hours working for and thinking about? Money. Consciously or unconsciously it's true.

There was his direct teaching to the Pharisees on giving. Then of course lots of parables on talents and minas and drachmas; others about land owners leasing out fields. There was one about a shrewd steward who invested or gave away other people's money. And of course there was great lesson for Peter on taxes when money was taken from the mouth of a fish. Who could think of this topic and not remember the feeding of the 5,000? Remember the statement of the apostles after Jesus said to them, "Oh, are these people hungry? You feed them." They responded, "Jesus, it would take a whole pile of money to feed all these people, and even if we had it, where would we get the food way out here?" I imagine him just laughing at them on the inside with a sad sentiment of "Don't you people understand who I am yet? Money is not even a consideration to my power. Sit down and I will show you." Wow! Of course the great comforting words of the Sermon on the Mount ring down through history. "Look at the birds of the air, and the lilies of the field...they neither toil nor spin, yet your heavenly father feeds and clothes them." Upon hearing these words do our hearts not cry out as the people of old, "Never a man spoke as this man, for he speaks as one having authority." In other words, he hit the nail right on the head. He spoke to the issues that they were facing and did so with piercing insight because he did talk a lot about money. People could relate.

Are we any different? Nearly every thought we think can be related to money somehow and it is always close at hand in our thinking.

This chapter will deal with the use of our money as it relates to several areas:

- Our attitude towards money.
- Money and faith or spirituality.
- Money and compromise.
- Money and marriage and decision making.
- Money and children and training them for fiscal sense and stewardship.
- Making money.
- Saving money.
- Spending money.
- Losing money.
- Spending too much money, i.e. debt
- Giving money.
- Making major purchases.

The list could go on and on. The fact is that money is a very important part of our lives. It touches our families, our relationship with our children, our future, our decision making process, and just about everything in our lives including even our health. In this chapter I am going to use the term money loosely. I am referring also to commerce and trade. Anything really related to business and the market place as well as wealth and assets in general. The purpose of this chapter is not a systematic biblical treatise on finances, giving, or stewardship, but it is a *"thinking out loud together"* about our finances and our revenue generating activities (our jobs and our businesses) and how they relate to our family and our children.

I will also be sharing personal experiences. I want to restate that these are *our* experiences and you do not have permission to make them normative unless the Holy Spirit tells you so. Fair enough?

A healthy perspective on money: two points will suffice here.

1. Little pieces of paper with numbers on it.
2. Don't take it too seriously.

That's right. It's only money! Say it out loud. "It's only money." Ouch, did that hurt? Money is such a source of tension isn't it? It creates tension in marriage, tension in families, tension in churches, and tension in governments—all over money. Tension leads to conflict; conflict leads to combat—lots of people fighting and dying over these little pieces of paper with numbers on them. It's sad.

I believe that God wants us to trust him for his provision for us so we don't have to worry so much about money. This affects us in big and little ways. I've seen my wife stew over missing a sale, or not getting the best deal in the department store or grocery store. You buy an item at full price that was half price last week. What was a good day is now ruined.

We've got to start seeing God in the little details. We all suffer little financial losses, some due to carelessness and others just happen. I remember not long ago that the girls used my heavy duty tow rope to pull a car out of the snow. When they were done, they left it on the hood of the car and when they got back, it was gone. Re-tracing our steps did not reveal it. It was a nice one and cost 40 bucks. I was a little ticked. My wife was furious at the girls and let them have it. Okay, it was a loss, a preventable one, a teachable moment, but it's only money. We can always buy a new one, or do without it (as we have). It's not important enough to destroy the kids over it.

Gabrielle came out to greet me in the driveway when I rolled in from work in my pickup as she usually does. She's on the running boards before the truck stops. Wanting to help she grabbed the gallon of milk in the back seat. Two seconds later it was flying across the driveway on the ice and milk was flying everywhere. I grabbed it and held it upside-down, away from the crack, to save what I could while I sent her inside to get a pitcher to put the remainder in. I am not going to get too excited about it. Sure, milk is $4 per gallon. I nearly went into cardiac arrest when I discovered that, but I am not going to destroy the child who was trying to help. Did I use it as a teachable moment? You bet. In the final analysis, it's only money.

Can't God do with our money whatever he wants to? If he wants to take away my tow rope and give it to someone else, isn't that his business? What is he trying to say to me through this?

We all have bad things happen to us where we experience financial losses. I had a friend who lost the lower unit of his boat on a rock to the tune of a few thousand dollars. Ouch. We always have to ask, "God, what are you trying to teach me through this?" We can't ruin relationships over money. Sometimes we have to count our losses and move on.

One year we lost $30,000 in two poor business deals, back-to-back. It was a tough thing because it was for work performed, for which we were not paid. We really needed the money and the boys worked hard, too, for an entire summer so it was their loss, too. What can we do? Sue someone? Possibly. I chose to forget it. Both incidents. Cut my losses and move on. When I see these guys in town in the grocery store my blood doesn't boil anymore because God allowed it to happen and it's only money. This can be a healthy perspective to get us on to forgiving.

Also, I am reminded about the lessons we learned as we went through these ordeals. The boys, my wife, all of us learned a lot. Education costs money, no matter how you get it. You can pay by the credit hour or by the school of hard knocks, but pay me now or pay me later.

One great scripture that carried us through those times is the verse, "in all labor there is profit." That's God's word and I chose to believe it. Sure the world would look on and say, "Come on Paul, you worked all summer and there was no profit because it was withheld. In reality we profited immensely through the lessons learned. David and Daniel, my teenage partners, were like the sons of thunder, "Turn us loose Dad…. Let's get an attorney…I can't believe we just walked away from that." They were good business lessons for young entrepreneurs in the making. It was rather funny because as much as two years later when we were contemplating buying a new car or some needed business equipment, David would say something like "Sure would be nice to have an extra 20 grand right now Dad. If we got paid from so and so we could have the item free today." I would just give him my big smile.

I also realized that five years from this event, David would be training to be an attorney. He knows first hand what it's like to be a victim. He knows what it's like to work all summer and lose money and not get paid. I think this lesson in his formative years is going to be very much a milestone in his life and legal career.

I need to say that at the time, $30,000 was more than we had ever been able to save, so it was a deep lesson and a significant one. We had undertaken a huge remodeling project, i.e. we tore our house down and moved into the basement with 9 children, and believe me, we could have really used the money.

It took us almost two years to recover from those losses at a great sacrifice to our entire family.

We realized that all wealth is from him and to him, and he gives us power to gain wealth, so in the final analysis, don't sweat it, they're only pieces of paper with numbers on it. But there is another perspective that we also need to catch.

Part of this thinking is really the practical outflow of the idea that all that I have comes from God. It's healthy, it's liberating, and it's powerful.

1. **Money is sacred since it is a representation of the investment of time.**

When you think about it, money is an exchange for someone's time—mine or someone else's—so it therefore is sacred. Now I know that this is the opposite concept of the above principle, but both none-the-less are true. [As a side note, we must always remember that for nearly every spiritual principle there is usually an equal and opposite spiritual principle so the necessity of walking in the Holy Spirit is even more essential.]

This is a truth that we must grasp and teach our children. The passing of a dollar represents an exchange of part of your life. What did you have to do to earn that dollar? And what are you really giving when you hand that piece of paper with numbers on it to the cashier?

As a boy I had a paper route. I made about five cents per paper delivered. So if something cost me a dollar I would do a little mental gymnastics and say "Hey, that candy bar is worth 20 papers. Now if I have to ride my bike from Mrs. Slipkowski's house to Charlie Nutter's to deliver 20 papers, that represents about 15 minutes. Then I would think of walking that route on a cold snowy New England day and often I would be deterred from buying something because the sacrifice in real terms was just too great.

When the kids were young, 6 to 10 years old, we got a paper route. Judy would drive them at 5 a.m. before I even got up or went to work, and David also had an afternoon route for years. He also learned to do the "How many papers will this cost me?" routine.

Rarely should we give our children money but teach them to work for it.

The key element in this principle is that money should not be squandered frivolously on foolish stuff or silly entertainment. My kids freak out when they see their friends putting two, three, and as much as twenty dollars in a vending machine that catches toys at a local mall when traveling with friends. They come home and, with eyes as big as baseballs, tell me about some kid dumping twelve dollars into this machine like they've never seen anything so stupid in all their lives. My 11-year-old is laughing at her friend and saying, "I wouldn't pay a dollar for the thing if I could buy it outright, never mind twelve dollars to try and win it." She can't imagine someone being so frivolous and wanting to buy something so stupid. I had to laugh because what she doesn't realize is that this is the way that most kids spend their money. It burns a hole in their pockets for momentary pleasures. Sadly, these kids grow up to be adults with spending habits and self-gratification habits that are out of control. It starts young, so it's important to lay a foundation while they are young.

Another important application of this principle is that we must learn the value of sacrifice and delayed gratification. If we want something, we've got to sacrifice to get it. That's the way life is. Saying yes to something means saying no to something else. If the kid wants a baseball glove, he needs to say no to a hundred candy bars. If he wants a motorcycle, he needs to say no to a baseball glove and a trip to the amusement park, and several other items on his list of desires and impromptu wishes. Life is about sacrifices.

We can't just have what we want today. We've got to work at it and learn to be content without it. We learn the value of things when we realize how long we took to acquire that item. Contentment is essential.

We lived in our basement for two years because we didn't have the money to continue construction and continue to fund our growing business at the same time. We had to make choices and those choices meant that our personal comforts came last, after business and necessities. We drove old cars for many years. We buy hand-me-down clothes from the good will, we grow a garden and can food, all sacrifices so that we can do other things with the limited resources that we do have. So we need to cultivate contentment and sacrifice; delayed gratification. We do without today, so we can have something better tomorrow.

This thinking too flows out of the understanding that life is sacred and we can't have and do everything so we need to be wise in the judicious use of our resources.

2. Money is a good thing to have, so make all that you can.

Now any truth can be twisted and abused and this is one that easily could. The concept is an important one when we consider doing great things for God. Whatever we do it usually requires money, so it stands to reason, that the more we have, the more we can do. (If we are wise and can handle the resources as God gives them to us.)

Given the choice of being poor or being rich, I think I'll choose being rich. Well you didn't spend the money on this book for someone to tell you that! There is however a false piety that says that being poor is good and that if one is rich then they are somehow immoral or dishonest or crooked in some way.

Now I don't teach and believe a prosperity Gospel as such. But I do know that Job was one of the richest men in the world at the time of his demise. Abraham was a wealthy man and owned lots of animals, and servants, and they are still fighting over his land! Matthew was a tax collector and Luke was a physician.

The thing we want to emphasize is that maximizing one's earning potential is essential to being a provider and a bread winner for the family. We have a right and a duty and responsibility to make as much money for our families as is practical without compromise, dishonesty, or greatly shirking our responsibilities. I say greatly shirking them because anyone who's owned a business has had to work long hard hours and knows what it's like to 'do what you have to do' sometimes to keep the business going.

What we shouldn't do is compromise our convictions or moral standards to make more money. Doing things that are illegal or spiritually unhealthy may offer the prospect of immediate financial advances, but will not pan out in the end, because God will not bless it. Also, keeping in the forefront of our thinking the spiritual needs of our family and their need to have a Papa in the home are important things to keep in mind when considering company promotions, increased responsibilities, and family moves.

One little phrase that has helped me over the years is this: "Saying yes to someone means saying no to someone else." That someone else is usually my wife and kids. When someone wants me to throw in something for free, sure I can do it. I can say "This is a chance to minister to this person, to be a good Christian and help them out." The problem with this is that down the line I might be saying "No, honey we can't" ... do such and such or we can't finish the house, or send the kids to piano lessons, etc.

So we have to understand that acquiring resources is a good thing

I have always liked the verse that says, "By wisdom a house is built. By understanding it is established, and by knowledge its rooms are filled with all precious and pleasant riches." It takes a lot to build a house and establish it (i.e. get it paid for) and then make it nice. This is something that everyone can admire and respect. This is one of those things that is "good in the sight of all men" as the scripture says.

Since we have a large family and are often accused of "bringing all these kids into the world" and "overpopulating the planet," and having "all these mouths to feed" (as if there were kids lining the foyer when I walked in all like little birds with their mouths open and waiting for crumbs to be thrown to them), I have always been conscious about making sure they are well provided for. I don't want the name of my God slandered because his hand is too short to provide for a few kids and their many needs. Further, I have always desired to make enough money and resources to have something to share.

Ephesians says, "Let him who steals steal no longer, but let him labor performing with his own hands what is good so he may have something to share with him who has needs." So when we plant a garden, we plant lots extra to bring to church and share with friends. When we make money we want to have enough to meet basic needs and even give out and beyond ourselves. We want to be givers, and not just takers.

On the same note, I am an employer. I cannot pay my employees what I do not have. I need to make wages, cover my overhead, and make a profit. I tell my people, "I've never gotten a good wage from a poor man, guys. If I am not making money you surely are not going to." I cannot provide benefits, profit sharing, or bonuses if we don't have the money. So I've got to be the best steward I can be not only for my family, but also for my company and employees' sakes.

It was John Wesley who said, "Make all you can, save all you can, so you can give all you can." The making part is the first thing.

Three practical points: #1. Start a business. #2. Start a business. #3. Start a business. Have I made my point? Gather the family and start a family business. Do SOMETHING! It's great if it makes money but it's okay even if it doesn't. Think how much you will learn! You'll have a great experience, some fun stories to tell to future generations, and if nothing else, a big tax write-off. Believe it or not, sometimes losing money is necessary to get ahead in this world so the government doesn't come in and take it. Find something someone in the family is passionate about and do it. More on this topic below

3. Making Money is a fantastic tool for education.

I have already recounted the story of the paper routes and how they helped us instill financial sense into the children. This was not just some academic idea, but came out of my own experience as a youth.

I got my first paper route at 8 years old. I was in business. I was a little business man. I always had money, literally. I used to loan my parents money for bills and even remember loaning my parents $100 at 10 years old when they were going to the casino, of all places, in Atlantic City. As a youth I always had money to buy books, magazine subscriptions, candy and food, and whatever I really wanted. I kept that paper route for eight whole years, until I was 16 years old. I had grown it to nearly three times the size, but most importantly it taught me character. EVERY DAY, without fail, in rain or snow or blistering heat, between three and five o'clock for eight years, from 7 to

15 years old, I was delivering newspapers! To me this was an incredible adventure in my formative years.

I had weekly contacts with 35-50 families. I knew them all by name, went in and visited with them frequently, knew their unique needs and personalities. I learned more about psychology and sociology in those eight years than I could ever learn in a course at school. This also led to a clientele for odd jobs on occasions including some lawn mowing and raking. It was a great experience.

Then at age 15 I sold my first business (my paper route) to a kid up the street and got a job at a restaurant, the International House of Pancakes, busing tables. It was about 10 miles away, so I would ride my bike every day to work, get off at midnight, and ride it back home. By this time I was in high school and I worked 40 hours a week during my high school years. I was promoted to cook and then to a crew chief, and at 17 I was responsible for the entire restaurant. I would work Thursday and Sunday nights 4 p.m. to midnight, and Friday and Saturday nights 4 p.m. to 4 a.m. To this day I can't believe it. But it really was my salvation in many ways.

I got involved in the drugs and party scene not long after my parents divorced at age 13-14. When my friends and brother were going out to party on Friday and Saturday nights, I couldn't because I had to work.

I also remember that when the bars would close at 2 a.m. across the parking lot, the entire bar would migrate over to the restaurant and continue their festivities. Many a night I had to go out there and, at 17 years old, play bouncer and tell those guys if they didn't leave the waitresses alone I was going to have to call the cops. One night we did call the cops and the guys at the table jumped the cops and a big fight broke out right in the building. The police maced the whole restaurant and people flew out of there like wasps out of a nest without paying their bills to escape the tear gas. It was a lot of responsibility for a young kid, but at 15 I welcomed it and it gave me purpose, seriousness, wisdom, and of course money.

I've done the same thing with my own children through the years. One year I challenged the kids to make some extra money by raking leaves. Since we home educate, we've got some freedom over our schedule, so every day at three o'clock we would go out and rake leaves. We ran a simple line ad. "Spring yard cleanup; call for a quote." The phone rang off the hook. I would go look at the job and quote then between 50 to 100 bucks depending on the lot size and we could do between two and four a day and I suppose we averaged $200 per day and it wasn't long before we made $4,000 and bought a good used family van with the money. The kids were ecstatic. They all, and mean all, pitched in and helped.

The little kids stood on the tarp as a ballast so the leaves could be raked on to the tarp and hauled off to the land fill. Everyone really learned how to hustle. We could blast out a city lot in half an hour with 8-12 people working. The kids invited some other home school kids along and they were glad to make some money too. So here we were working together as a family, having a good time, hiring others, and leaning how to hustle for a dollar.

Not long into this thing several of the customers asked, "Do you guys do lawns?" "No," I replied, "just spring cleanup." After several inquiries I began saying, "Yes we do and we're starting the first cut on May 14; would you like to sign up?" I pre-sold contracts all during April and May and bought a good used commercial mower on the 13th of May and stayed up converting an old flat bed trailer into a useable transport trailer and, as promised, on the 14th we were mowing lawns. Keep in mind this is a very rural area, not downtown Saint Paul, so this type of thing was really uncharted waters in these parts, but we discovered a need and came up with a plan to meet it.

It was a great summer. We worked our construction jobs all day and then would leave the jobsite with the hired hands around 3 p.m. and go mow lawns until dark at around 9 p.m. We still had baseball games to go to, but we had 26 accounts that we mowed every week. For a little side business a couple days a week, we grossed $20,000 that year. It was a lot of fun and the kids once again saw what we could accomplish when we worked together and put our minds to it.

One funny story I remember is when Daniel, who was our trim man (being lowest in seniority of course, got the hardest job), ran the trimmer around Maxine Moe's cute little tenderly cared for apple tree and commenced to peal the bark off it up about six inches so it looked like it was wearing a sock. She blew a gasket. It was a fun learning experience as we assured her the tree would not die and that if it did, we would replace it. We prayed over that tree every time we drove by and still laugh when we see it today. Another valuable lesson learned. But it gets better.

The next year we decided not to do the commercial lawn care so we only kept a handful of accounts, special people who we felt loyal to and of course the easy lawns that were real money makers, and we picked up one big resort. We were just too busy with our regular summer construction schedule and wanting to play baseball and not be so pressed. The following year we kept only the resort which was a $5,000 account in one place and we could drop off a couple of kids and it could be done in one day and it was real close to our house and on the way to town (God's hand of blessing). Well during this time I got a phone call from a property management firm in Texas, asking if we did home repairs. They found us on the internet by chance. Yes we did I told him and he explained that they managed properties that banks repossessed and needed to change the locks and winterize them and sometimes just recover the property on behalf of the bank. He inquired if we could assist him with a property right in our town. I told him we could and then he asked me. "Could you recommend a commercial lawn service in your area?" I think I actually had the trailer and the mower on my truck as he spoke, so I said, "Sure; we actually have a separate division of our company that does nothing but lawn care." Remember now, people like professionals with credentials and I assured him that we were actually licensed and insured and he was ecstatic. I didn't tell him it was my daughter Susan's turn to drive the rig this year because she just turned 16 (in our family that means you *must* get your license), and Daniel was now promoted to chief equipment operator because David was running construction crews.

But I did tell him that it wouldn't be worth our time or his money if he couldn't give us 12-16 properties so we could make a route and hit them all in one round each week. I think he gave us 28 properties from the Canadian border to the Iowa border, nearly a 7-hour span. So I did what any good father would do, I put my 16-year-old daughter in a pickup truck, gave her my credit card and her younger brother Daniel and the team departed. They had a map and a list but no directions or, of course, phone numbers, because the homes were vacant and repossessed. What an adventure and learning experience.

I sent them with a digital camera to take pictures and a check list to inspect the property if they could get in, and I emailed the pictures to the company in Texas of the before and after. I think we grossed 15 thousand off that account but more importantly, it was an incredible learning adventure for Daniel and Susan in their formative years and gave them wisdom and maturity beyond their years. It also forced them to be stretched and to work together. (I will save the story of the head gasket going out on the pickup down by Rochester, MN for another chapter.)

Being in business as a family is a lot of fun. Usually David, Daniel and I will be sitting around the living room at 10 p.m. after returning from our respective job sites and daily activities and sharing and swapping stories about customers and employees and we get going on some business plan or topic or idea and the creative juices are flowing and we are getting excited about something and usually disagreeing about the proper course of action. Then, in jest and half truth, we declare an official executive committee meeting whereby we need to round up Mom and Susan from the four corners of the house and get all the key players together to gather more field data to make our executive decisions. We have lots of laughs and the neat thing is that a simple phone call can begin a serendipitous adventure when we are willing to think outside the box and give God permission to work there in our lives if we let him.

4. Learn how to cry out to God for provision.

As a young man I went into the military at age 17, 10 days after graduating from high school. I joined the Army Corps of Engineers. Our motto was "If we can't do it, it can't be done!" You know, you don't go running around an army base yelling that fifty times a day without starting to believe it a little bit. I suppose that's the point of all the rah-rah-rah army mottos any way. So I have always been the type of person who is willing to try just about anything to begin with, so this stint with the Corps of Engineers only added fuel to my fire. Our little ditty motto went like this:

We, the unwilling, have done so much, with so little, for so long, that we are now qualified to do anything, with nothing! It's humorous, but when you see God work and you trust him to lead you, if you are not careful, this could become a way of life; a scary way of life. One in which you are definitely not in control. And in such cases, there is only one thing to do… Cry out to God.

When God leads you into something that is bigger than you and your abilities and your resources and your begged and borrowed resources, then there is nothing left to do but cry out to God. Like Moses standing with is back to the sea with the Egyptian army pressing in, there have been many times that I have been forced to cry out to God.

As I said, we have never been people of abundant means so there have always been occasions where we were crying out to God for provision of a project coming on line, or for the kids to get accepted in school, for babies who need to be delivered, for payroll that needs to be paid, for the big stuff and the little stuff.

God is there for us in all of it. Nahum 2:2 tells us that "The Lord is good, a stronghold in the day of trouble and he knoweth them that trusteth in him."

What a great verse. He *is* good. He desires our blessing if we would only make ourselves available to receive it. He delights in being our stronghold and he knows when we leave the reefs of personal comfort and cast ourselves upon him and his mercy in the sea of uncertainty and potential loss. He has never let us down.

Have we miscarried children? Yes. Have we experienced hardships and financial struggles? Yes, but God has always shown himself strong and done "over and exceedingly abundant and beyond all that we have asked or thought, according to his power that is at work in us" (see Ephesians 3:19).

We need to learn how to cry out to God for his provision.

It's really quite simple. You don't need to teach a baby how to cry out, they will do it naturally.

One year we brought our then only six children to the amusement park. The triplets were very young and as we made our way through the crowd I warned the kids to stay close to mommy and daddy. Daniel was a happy and independent three year old and soon wandered off by himself. What he didn't know was that I was following him from about 20 feet away watching him. He was going along enjoying himself and making good time. Soon he was looking around at all the people and scurrying around like a mouse on the floor at a crowded cocktail party. I kept my distance and watched. I watched his eyes as he began for the first time looking up all those pant legs for someone at the top who looked familiar. He went from person to person and then did something interesting, he started running. Where he was going I couldn't quite figure out but as he ran he turned to his left and without knowing it started running right towards me as I was walking parallel to him about 15 feet away through the crowd. Now he was coming right towards me but he was totally lost and for the first time he knew it. Then the magic moment happened. It only took a split second. As his little sprint trickled to a walk his eyes went back and forth wildly and I could see every expression on his face and read every thought in his mind. For the first time he realized that he was totally alone and completely lost. As his pace came to a close he rolled his head back and his brow began to wrinkle and his lip began to quiver and he was just about to cry out when through the crowd I said "Daniel." He looked through the crowd at me with a look of both relief and shame and I asked, "What's the matter?" As I walked towards him it gave him a few seconds to regain his composure and I said, "Did you get lost? Were you scared without mommy and daddy?" I scooped him up into my arms and brought him safely back to mommy and the rest of our party.

   Isn't that just like us? We are going through life thinking life is great when in reality we are only moments away from discovering or some circumstance of life reveals that we are completely lost and helpless to conditions beyond our control. Like Daniel, our first inclination is to scurry around and try to figure things out. We try to gain our bearing. Then sometimes in a panic, we run. Do we really think we're going to fix the problem by running? (It's like speeding when you are lost. You want to make up for lost time, but you don't know where you are going.)

Then the realization occurs to us that our current course of action is not helping and like Daniel we slow to a walk and then throw our heads back and cry out for God to help us. And then the magic moment happens. There he is! Through the crowd he is there. We didn't see him but he was walking right along beside us all the way. When we see him, we realize where we are and what we need to do to get back into his arms and back on the path that he wants for us.

O beloved how our heavenly father delights as we cry out to him and crumple into a heap right into his loving and everlasting arms. I cannot tell you how many times I've cried out to him and said like Moses, "If you don't go up with me I cannot go. Show me thy presence and thy glory. This people are too great for me and their burdens too numerous and besides, they are *thy* people." Let me tell you one incident.

We were living in Connecticut in the late 80s and early 90s when a serious recession hit—300 thousand people moved out of the state and headed for the Carolina's and Georgia. People who had bought second homes as rentals and investment properties were starting to lose everything. There was a sense of apprehension in the air as the economy tottered. I was self-employed and couldn't find work—at all, anywhere. My health insurance just went up to over $500 per month, and my monthly rent was $750, which was a lot of money then. So I needed $1,250 within days just to keep things going, and we were broke. I think we had a couple of hundred dollars left to our name, basically a pocket full of milk money. To make matters worse, Judy and I really wanted to attend a Home Schooling Convention down in Tennessee that we felt the Lord wanted us to attend and would be a blessing. The cost of the convention would be close to $2,000 by the time we got done with registration, meals, lodging, travel, and of course those few extra things you need to buy while you are camping. I would be gone for nearly two weeks with travel including two days down and two days back, driving nearly straight through. So that meant that when I got back I would need another month's rent and insurance and of course all the monthly bills would be due for both months. The conference was only 10 days away. Where was I going to come up with about $5,000 in the next 10 days when I couldn't even find work for minimum wage?

    I was praying hard about this and crying out to God. "God if you want us to go to this conference you've got to do something – fast. Please help me. Show me your way." Since I didn't have any work, I decided to go over to the chapel and fix the panic door hardware on the gym door that I had installed some months ago on our Christian school building. I took a shortcut to the chapel over Rocky Top Road and as I went a saw a man up on his roof, about a quarter of a mile from our home. He was on a ladder on the roof hung over the ridge with a makeshift cleat and he was 'painting' his asphalt shingled roof with pitch. He was covered with it and it was a hot day. I didn't know whether to feel sorry for the guy or to laugh at him. I explained to him that I lived up the street and that I was a roofer and just happened to have a hole in my schedule right now and could give him a good price if he wanted to do it right away on Monday morning (this happened on a Friday). This guy was a true Yankee if I ever met one. He went on to explain to me that he had put that roof on twenty-five years ago (it was a 20-year-shingle), and when it needed replacing he would be the one to do it. Seeing the circumstances, I kicked my salesmanship into high gear and told him how painless it would be to go down inside the house and have a glass of lemonade and let us do the work for him. A man of his age and stature, being a wise businessman and landowner, shouldn't do this kind of work, it really is the worst of the worst, and it's dangerous too. Don't you want to enjoy your retirement years?

I explained to him that my family and I were going on vacation to Tennessee in 10 days and due to unfortunate circumstances other work I was planning on fell through and I just happened to have the next week open. Since he was just down the road we could tear this puppy off and have her buttoned up by Friday with all the mess cleaned up and he could enjoy his summer. I pulled out a business card and wrote $8,000 on the card. I told him normally I'd charge $12,000 for this roof but because I had this week open I would give him a good deal. I really needed to know today because I had to order shingles and plan the work for next week. He thanked me, put the card in his pocket and assured me that he was going to do the job himself if and when it needed it. I said to myself "I thought I had seen it all." As I left I said, "Please sir, don't think about calling me when I get back because summer will be in full swing and I may not be able to get to it and of course I could not give you the discount that I've offered you today."

I went to the chapel and fixed the door. Later that night we were having homemade pizza and visiting with friends, it was our Friday night tradition, when the phone rang. It was this guy and he said he wanted me to do the roof. I told him great I would be right over after dinner to sign a contract and pick up a check. The check would be for $4,000 dollars, half down and half on completion. When I got off the phone we did a little dance, some high fives and said, "Tennessee, here we come. Thank you, Father."

God had done the impossible. He had provided exactly what we needed, when we needed it, over and above what we needed actually because we even had enough to pay utilities, taxes, next month's food and of course giving. God is faithful. He showed himself strong because we were trusting in him. My statements to the homeowner were true. I *was* going to be busy that summer and I *was* going to go to Tennessee, and I *really did* need a check today to get that roof in my schedule for next week. I was operating in faith and trusting in my heavenly Father. God is faithful and we need to learn to cry out to him. When we do, serendipitous things can happen if we are willing to think outside the box.

Before we leave this topic of crying out to God for provision and direction, I would like to share one more story that took place during a subsequent year in Connecticut.

The economy ground almost to a halt; I couldn't find work again. There were 450 units of apartment being built literally right in my backyard and because of Mexican labor I couldn't even get a day's work. In desperation I agreed to trim out an entire house for $80. Hey I had mouths to feed. After carrying 9 doors across the complex to the third floor, and then all the trim and baseboard and chair rail, I only got about half of it done in a day, working like a maniac and I figured if I really hustled I could trim a three bedroom unit in one day. (Okay, so I am an optimist, I admit it.) So I figured it was going to take me two days, but the worst part is that I had to leave a couple thousand dollars worth of tools in the place while I stocked the units so I figured if one nail gun gets clipped at 350 bucks I am going to be coming up way short. So I quit and never even went back to try to collect.

The next day I walked into a wood manufacturing plant right up the street because I was getting desperate and needed food money and something was better than nothing. A gruff plant supervisor named Dave with a voice like a bullfrog, a big beard, and a frame like a linebacker handed me a clip board and said "Fill this out." When I asked how much the position paid he said five dollars per hour. Two weeks ago I had employees that I was paying 12 and 14 an hour and my health insurance alone was over $500 per month. I started the mental calculations. "I could work here all month and barely pay my medical insurance," I thought. Dave reentered the room and with a booming voice that quite startled me right out of my ponderings, "Are you gonna fill that out or just stand there?" Without even thinking about it I sat down and started filling out the application all the while saying to myself, "Why am I doing this? I can't believe I am doing this! I have my own company. I am self-employed! On a good day I could make more in one hour than I could make here in a whole day. What's going on here Lord?" When I handed the clipboard back to Dave he looked it over and asked me when I could start. I explained to him my situation and that I really could only work part-time and temporary because I needed some income while I was looking for other work. He agreed to let me work from 6 to 11 a.m., which would give me five hours a day and still be done early enough to do estimates and visit jobsites and try to hustle up some other work.

So began my serendipitous adventure at Amendola General Woodwork. I started the next morning on the assembly line packing parts, whistling, singing under the din of the machinery and enjoying the sights and sounds of a new market place and anticipating what adventures the Lord would have for me in my new career as a minimum wage factory worker. About the third day we had a company employee meeting to discuss health insurance benefits and I met the owner of the company, a young feller in his early 40s who was running the business that his father had started back in the 50s. After the meeting, being the shy type that I am, I decided to introduce myself to the gentleman and make my services available to him. It also so happened that as I was investigating insurance policies for my own employees, I had learned some things and passed that information along to him, which ended up being a benefit to the company and saving them a lot of money since they had some 50 employees. I told him that I had fallen into some hard times and if he had any construction work he needed done or knew of anyone who did to please let me know. It just so happened that the pocket door in his home had been off the tracks for quite some time and his wife had recently been bugging him to do something about it so he dispatched me to fix it for him, which I promptly did, that afternoon.

The house was a beautiful New England traditional salt box style house with all solid cherry floor through out and white painted trim. It was impressive. I managed to get the trim off the door without even breaking the miter joints and I glued it back in place after fixing the door so the owner was pleased and impressed and said "How did you do that?" Apparently the casings must have been pre-splined or they would not have held together so well and I replied with a little smile, "just little tricks of the trade I guess." This little event and circumstance began a lasting friendship and business relationship that was an amazing adventure from the Lord.

"When Armand recognized my talents he gave me several maintenance projects to work on which I really needed. I met the father and mother who were wonderful people and put all new floors in their house. I started a counseling ministry with Dave and the other shop supervisor, the number two man, and was able to share Christ with several people on the line.

A new assembly line was being set up and Armand asked me if I would consider coming on full time to work as the maintenance guy/engineer to set up the whole thing. He agreed to pay me $25 per hour on the payroll, so this was a good wage, and the plant was literally one quarter of a mile away from my house. I could even go home for lunch. It was interesting learning about automation and setting up this line. I enjoyed it and it was a great provision for my household. This promotion came about a week after I was there. Had I not been willing to take a menial job and allow the Lord to lead I would never have met all these people and got this additional employment at such a critical time, and so close to home. But it gets better.

I invited Armand, the owner, out for lunch one day and we developed a wonderful mutual friendship. I had a set of triplets and he had twins that were about five years older than mine so it was really a fun and natural thing and we encouraged each other. Right at the time this was all happening, Armand was just beginning a spiritual awakening. I simply steered him toward Jesus as THE higher power and to the Word and God continued to mature Armand in his new found faith. He has since become a member of Fellowship of CEO's for Christ and hosts meetings and Bible studies and is on fire for his faith in Jesus. PTL. But there's more.

Armand came to me one day and asked me if I would be interested in helping him start a third shift because the overseas orders were increasing and we were picking up accounts in Germany and China and we needed a third shift in order to make production. I thought about it and after discussing it with Judy said 'Sure, why not." You see, my main vocation was a preacher. I preached about 40 Sundays a year while working to support my family so it didn't really matter what I did as long as it paid the bills and gave me the freedom to respond to the Lord and keep me freed up for ministry opportunities.

We started a third shift and the highlight was hiring a young black girl named Andrea. She was a mom and happily married and just wanting to make some extra money for the family so she worked nights while hubby watched the kids. It wouldn't be forever, but for now it worked. I could relate to that. (Isn't all of life somewhat temporary anyway? Once you grab on to something too tightly we lose it.) Andrea had a three-year-old named Christian. I had just purchased and read the beautifully illustrated children's edition of John Bunyan's classic tale, *The Pilgrim's Progress*. I brought the book to her so she could read it to the child and I knew it would be cool for the little guy to be the hero of the story in living color. Well you guessed it, in a matter of time Andrea and her husband became believers and months later after I had left the company she called the secretary and got my address and sent me a nice note explaining how I "led her and her husband to the Lord" and how grateful she was.

After we got the new line installed and the third shift up and running we turned it over to someone else and once again I was on my own. It was a neat adventure and I kept in touch with my new friend Armand, and I would call him and we would get together for lunch and disciple each other as he would ask me about my finances and how I was doing with work, and I would hold him accountable for getting into the word and bringing his family to church. It was a very mutually satisfying relationship because we both admired and respected each other. He respected me because I was able to teach him a few things about his spirituality and I admired him because he was young and rich and a CEO and was filling big shoes in the marketplace. It was fun helping him by being his sounding board and being introduced to the decision-making processes that he was facing, something that I was about to find out about first hand, real soon.

During lunch one day he described a difficult situation with his current office manager, who happened to be a female. She had developed a passive aggressive relationship with him and was a constant source of irritation to him. He said "Paul I've got to fire her, but I can't replace her… I don't know what to do!" I agreed that she had to go and I offered my services. "Do it; let her go today after lunch. I'll start tomorrow as your new office manager and keep things afloat until we interview and hire someone better." We just looked at each other and laughed hysterically. God had sent me back to him just when he needed me and it was another adventure for me. I started the next morning as the office manager, and receptionist, back on the payroll this time answering phones, doing payroll, calling on customers and lining up interviews with bookkeepers. I learned all about running a business quickly. I had four days to figure out how to do payroll on a complicated and dysfunctional multi-component, proprietary accounting software for almost 50 employees. It was a crash course in business management and introduction to things like margins and mark up, and inventory, cost accounting, accounts payable and receivable, earned discounts, and interest payments, spreadsheets and aging reports. I didn't do too badly for a rookie. We interviewed Joan a few weeks later and hired her, and I stuck around for a couple of weeks until we got the accounts stabilized and things in working order. Armand, Joan, and I really had a lot of camaraderie as we sought to pull all these things together and I was very fulfilled in being used of God to see it happen. Not to mention that I was paid a very good salary for something that I thoroughly enjoyed and had little or no formal training or experience for.

As I look back, it's somewhat of a modern day Joseph story. I came in at the basement level and in a few days I was working for Potiphor. I remember Armand going on vacation for a week to Disney World with his family because he had made the plans to go before all this stuff came down and he couldn't really get out of it. We had things just under control enough for him to get away and not worry about things. We even had to overnight the payroll checks down to him and back so we could pay the guys on Friday. I sat in the driver seat, right at the owner's desk, while he was away and just thought this is insane. A year ago I was hired here as a minimum wage assembly line employee, and now I am running the company. Yes, God is able to allow serendipitous things to happen in our lives as we learn to think outside the box in our walk with him.

5. **Have lofty goals and keep your eyes above the horizon.**

One of the passages that has always intrigued me is Ephesians 3:14-20, one of Paul's many awesome prayers for God's people. Slow down and stroll your way through each verse and savor the richness.

14 For this reason, I bow my knees before the Father, 15 from whom every family in heaven and on earth derives its name, 16 that he would grant you, according to the riches of his glory, to be strengthened with power through his Spirit in the inner man; 17 so that Christ may dwell in your hearts through faith; and that you, being rooted and grounded in love, 18 may be able to comprehend with all the saints what is the breadth and length and height and depth, 19 and to know the love of Christ which surpasses knowledge, that you may be filled up to all the fullness of God.

20 Now to him who is able to do exceeding abundantly beyond all that we ask or think, according to the power that

works within us, 21 to him be the glory in the church and in Christ Jesus to all generations forever and ever. Amen. (NAS)

Let's begin with verse 16. The foundation of God's blessing in our lives comes out of the richness of his glory. God is very rich and very full of glory. One of the Old Testament words for glory means fat, or full, or abounding in fullness. God possesses all things and all attributes and it is out of his fullness that he gives to us. We cannot underestimate this fact and it is one we must ponder, the fullness and the sufficiency of God. It is out of this fullness that Paul bestows a blessing upon the Ephesian believers and upon all of God's children who are wont to lay hold of it.

The opportunity before us is to be *strengthened with power through his spirit in our inner man.* That means staying power and overcoming power. God gives us the power to stay in the game and overcome the obstacles. He wants to give us this power in our inner man, the secret real you and me who deep down inside of us makes the hard decisions and fights the spiritual battles of doubt, worry, anger, lust, and the host of things that come against us. What a wonderful promise available to us—an unlimited supply of internal resources. It gets better.

He wants us to comprehend the immensity of his love for us. I think more often than not the heart of God breaks because we doubt his love. Like Jesus who wept before Jerusalem because of her unbelief and because of the loss of blessings that she missed as a result. I think we lose a lot of blessings because we really don't trust God in real and practical ways. He has them all lined up and waiting for us, but we choose a different path and as a result they have to sit on the shelf because we are unworthy to receive them.

I think that this will be one of the great judgments against us as believers at the judgment seat of Christ. It's only conjecture, but I think Jesus is going to show us the storeroom of blessings that we didn't receive while we clung to our wood, hay and stubble. The scripture says we will suffer loss. There are few things worse than regret. How about missing a good deal? You had it right there and you passed it up. I think that is how it's going to be in heaven. We will not be judged for our sin, because Jesus paid for that, but our works will judge ourselves and we will either hear well done, or we will realize ourselves those things that were otherwise.

Things really kick into high gear in this prayer as Paul revs his way up to verse 20 as he begins with the superlatives. "Now to him who is able to do **exceeding abundantly beyond all that we ask or think**, according to the power that works within us." Ponder those words. Exceedingly, abundantly, beyond ALL that we *ask* OR *think*. I am at a loss for words. How can you elaborate on exceedingly, abundantly and beyond? Was Paul talking pie in the sky religion? Was he preaching a prosperity Gospel? This is the guy who got his back beat raw numerous times, was stoned by angry mobs, sat in dirty prisons with criminals, and was shipwrecked and stranded at sea more than once. What was he talking about? Three things I believe were in his focus.

All of this suffering would have been worth it just to see the Lord Jesus face to face. Think of Paul's experience of being caught up into the seventh heaven. He was focusing on the "things that eye has not seen nor ear heard, that have not entered into the heart of man that God has prepared for those who love him.

I believe he was also contemplating the power of God that came to him in his prison cell where he and Silas began singing the praises of God through their parched throats and the agony of their wounded backs. Or the presence of Christ that came to him while floating on a piece of wood in the middle of the sea. Or the comfort that came to him when the angel appeared to him and told him, "Don't worry Paul, I will be with you and of the ship we will lose none." These impartations of power and glory to Paul in themselves alone far exceeded any human experience imaginable.

This is something that is greatly lost today and without becoming too mystical I would turn our reader to the writings of the saints of old, like Hudson Taylor and David Brainerd in particular. They would say things like, I was meditating on such and such a verse and the presence of Christ became very real to them and laid hold of them in powerful ways that changed them forever. If you've ever experienced this you know what I am talking about. These kinds of experiences were strengthenings with power in the inner man. They were intuitive communications from God concerning the manifestation of His presence in the inner man. These were special anointings or visitations of the Presence of God to communicate His will and heart to His servant. And then I think there is a third.

The third is that God is ABLE to do.... This speaks of the future. Of things God is yet to do here in the here and now as we yield ourselves to him. These are things beyond anything we can imagine in terms of personal fulfillment, true peace, joy, blessing, and ministry. It's not likely that we will experience these things in our outward experience until we experience them in our inner man.

The point here is that we need to set our sights high. Get a bigger view of God and his power and resources. We can never experience outwardly what has not become an inward reality.

6. Cultivate generosity.

As we contemplate the area of finances as it touches our families and children, is the need and desire to cultivate generosity. We do this by holding on to resources loosely. It is easy to become self-absorbed and constantly focus on our needs.

Does anyone ever really think they are rich? Not really, unless they are actually quite well off, or super rich. The Bible defines a rich person as one who has food and clothing and a shelter from the elements. This is the basis of contentment. Without contentment, we cannot give. If we are constantly comparing ourselves to others and always looking to those who are just one level higher on the food chain, we will never be content and never give generously. Being generous and giving to others is an attitude towards money and things before it becomes an act. We must always evaluate how tightly we hold on to things: money, wealth, positions, power, and people. All that we have is a trust from God and we are only stewards.

We are by no means philanthropists, nor have we been people of much means. Both of our families were working class people who were always basically poor. As a child the divorce of my parents put our family on the welfare rolls so I know what it was like to get food stamps, public assistance, and wait in line at school to get a free lunch ticket every day. Being poor was not fun. Through the years we have always tried to give generously to our church, to various causes, and to people in need. We've paid rent for people, fixed their cars, bought groceries, and even shared the proceeds of our gardens. We have always been generous with our time too, serving at the local church. We've served on boards and committees and showed up at the church work days. Although we are a large family, with unending needs, we want the focus of our lives to be serving others and not just ourselves.

One incident I remember clearly was when our church was raising money for a building fund for the Christian school. We were home schooling and it was in those struggling years in Connecticut when our fledgling business was still fledgling quite forcefully. I happened to have a thousand dollars and said, "Hey honey I feel like we should give it to the church for the school." I was praying about the church and our involvement and really wanted my heart to be connected with the people in the totality of the work and not just in the programs I was interested in. I sensed the Lord was saying to me "Where your treasure is, there will your heart be also." So we gave the offering to the church for the school.

Generosity is a character quality that we wanted to develop in our children. Often times I would give a child a $100 bill to put in the offering plate. While the ushers were working their way up the aisles I would watch them open it up and look at the denomination. I just thought it was healthy for a little kid to give away a $100 bill. In my mind it reinforced the point that money is for using, and not for hoarding. It is a blessing to us and God meant it to be a blessing to others. Often times I would do the same for special offerings. You know how it is. The college singing group comes to your church to do a concert or a missionary speaks on a Wednesday night. Now you've already given a tithe, perhaps an offering above that, and now here is another need/opportunity. You could give nothing. You could give a dollar just to give something. You could throw in a five. Or you could say, "Wow, what a blessing that was; wouldn't it be cool to give a hundred? I really can't afford it, but God will supply." So I would write out a check for a hundred dollars and give it to one of the older ones, David, Susan, or Daniel because they would know that we've already given and that this is over and above and they would see the sacrifice. Also, they may know that we are trying to save for such and such, or that the AC just went out on the van so these types of things would make this sacrifice more sacrificial to them. It would be something that they gave as well. So I've done this because I wanted them to learn to be generous.

I remember one of my older children saying that so and so was going on a mission field and I think we should support them. "Oh," I said, "thank you; I'll pray about that." After discussing it with Judy we were in favor of it and I said to this child a few days later, "Did you have an amount in mind?" The amount suggested was a generous amount for which I was glad, and I had the same amount in my mind as I thought of it too. So it was good to see the freedom of the older ones to be concerned with giving and being a blessing to others and they felt the freedom to give out of the family coffers.

Generosity concerns more than just material possessions; it's an attitude of the heart that looks for needs in the lives of others. It may be shoveling the neighbors walk in the winter, letting someone bat first at the ball field, or giving of your time to help someone. It bothers me when I see Christian people hoarding things. We have to hoard it because "It's gotta last me." It is as if we have only a limited supply and God cannot ever give us any more. We can't ever throw anything away because wouldn't you know, I might need it some day! So our lives get cluttered up with stuff and we get choked out with too much clothes and junk and we effectively cut off the flow of blessing from God because we hoard.

We have received many offerings and donations over the years. We have received cash gifts (large ones too), cars, furniture, food, vacations, and the Lord knows we've gotten clothes. We are grateful for all the things the Lord has provided to us from the generosity of others. Being in a large family you need to have the grace to receive things. We have also learned first hand that it is better to give than receive and we felt it very important for our children to lean this lesson too.

We also have to learn that just because something is free doesn't mean we need it, or if several are offered they must all be received. Generosity means embracing things lightly and gently. Hoarding resources flows out of an attitude of poverty and does not flow out of the fullness that the Lord intended us to experience.

Before we leave this topic, let me say a word about savings. I mean the nest egg idea. I have never really had a savings account. Sure, we've collected up some money for purchases and rainy days, but it was always a temporary thing to hold in store until it was needed (which usually isn't very long). We even run a business without much of a cash reserve. In my younger years I gave away anything extra I had because I believed literally that I was investing in God's savings plans and was sending my rewards ahead so I could enjoy them when I get there.

I still feel that way pretty much, but realize that I have to be a good steward of the assets that God has entrusted to me and to make provision for those entrusted to my care. Things like making sure we have money to pay the tax man, maintaining positive cash flow for the business, and having a contingency for unexpected repairs are all part of being wise. Although I own assets, I still have not started saving for retirement. For some people, that's all they do is worry about their retirement. This too can be a worry trap.

Let's look at our final point in this section and it's closely related to generosity.

7. All for one and one for all.

Yes, it's the three musketeers. That was their motto. They all were committed to each other and vowed to guard each other. This has been our financial practice in our family. This may sound strange, but this is how it worked out. Now I really can't take any credit for this because I didn't sit down with my wife and a legal pad and plan this whole thing out, it's just the way it happened as a result of little decisions we made as we went. Here's how it worked.

When we got married, we became a team. There was one purse; just our money—not mine and hers; one checkbook. We made spending decisions mutually, for the most part. We didn't have any hard fast rules; we didn't need any. I read recently that a couple agreed to a $20 limit on unapproved purchases; anything else they would discuss together. As time went on they raised it to $50. I thought it was a good idea; it brought unity and kept them from fighting while keeping their spending under control.

So we had one pot and one purpose and we all worked together for the good of the family. When we had needs we all drew out of the one.

When we made resources, it all went into the family fund.

As a result, we never paid our children for working for us in our businesses. Not when we were raking leaves, mowing lawns, or working carpentry and building houses. They never drew a paycheck, but worked for the family business. Incidentally, until recently I never drew a paycheck either. Whatever money was left at the end of the job was mine and so we all worked to maximize that bottom line.

As needs arose those needs were met. When the kids turned 16, they were given a car to drive any time they needed to. If they wanted to go to town and play hockey with their friends, I would give them the keys and 20 bucks. If I felt that they were on the run too much, I would say, "No, I don't think so; not tonight." These guys were 18 and 20! If they wanted to go skiing, I gave them the keys to the suburban and a hundred bucks and said, "Have a good time."

Susan worked full time as a bookkeeper in our company office and never drew a paycheck. David and Daniel worked full time in the field on crews doing manual labor from 12 to 20 and never drew a paycheck. This was obviously of significant financial impact to our business since we could retain capital and begin building with cash and not on debt. The sacrifice of their labor made that happen.

Our kids had a lot of responsibility and a lot of resources. We pretty much gave them their own credit cards with complete access to all of our accounts and assets at about 17 years old. There was no question about their responsibility and compared to their peers they had a much better deal, and so did I. They didn't ask for a lot and I didn't have to say no too often. They had the same goals as I did, to get my house paid off, pay down on some equipment, and solidify the financial foundation of our business. They were truly partners, even though I had the final say.

One day David came to me and he and Daniel were eyeing a boat on the internet. We already had a speed boat so I wasn't keen on another one. They wanted a bigger one so they could wake board and parasail. I vetoed the idea. Later I got to thinking about it and actually prayed about it. It started to make sense. We were a big family and definitely cannot fit into one boat. If we have friends or relatives over it would take forever to ski everyone and just shuttling people back and forth to the island would take all day. The boys were getting older and more independent and going for the day without the family to special lakes or with their friends or just the older kids would be okay and I could take time with the little girls who need time and attention and who would be afraid of the water, etc. We almost had two separate families with different needs, so that purchase seemed to make more sense. After all, there is always a resale value and the time spent with the kids and them spending time with each other is always a good investment.

It was a few days later when Daniel found a good deal on the internet for a nice speed boat in the state of New Jersey. He told me what a good deal it was on eBay and it was going off in 24 hours and I had better pray about it, as he gave me the special wink. It was effectively a cross between pulling rank on me and starting a coup. I knew they really wanted the boat so after discussing it with Judy we said, "Sure, go for it." So I got a ten thousand dollar money order out of the bank and sent them to New Jersey to pick up their new boat. I was really proud of them. The delayed gratification of their youth paid off because at 19 David had his own boat, paid cash for it, and I put it in his name. He had sacrificed and worked hard (remember working all summer for free), and now it was paying off. I was proud of him. I was proud of my God who is able to do exceedingly abundantly above and beyond all that we ask or think. I thought of his contemporaries and the kids at church; they were working at the local gas station for wages and David was buying a $10,000 boat. I thought of where I was at 18 and that I had never even seen $10,000 all at once until I was about 27 years old!

The family dynamics as a result of this were amazing. As one needed music lessons, or new violins to the tune of about a thousand bucks a piece, we all realized that we were all working for these things to the blessing of the person receiving it, whatever their need was. This eliminated a lot of selfishness. We would see other families fighting about who used the car last and who's responsible to put 10 bucks worth of gas in it now. When the kids have their own jobs and their own money, it makes for a bit of selfishness and develops the idea that we are all individuals here and we're all in it for ourselves.

My children have use of the family vehicles and unlimited gas as long as what they are doing is an approved trip or activity, which usually means running a younger sibling to a sporting event or music lesson, or doing something work related. We never let our kids just go hang out with friends. Everything has to have a purpose.

When it came time for college or mission trips, the younger ones are now working to put the older ones through college and keep Susan on the mission field. Hopefully as the older ones graduate and start their own families, they will be able and desirous of helping some of the younger ones with college tuitions and missions trips. I'm not expecting them to do this, but with the spirit of selflessness that prevails, I could not imagine them not helping if they have the means.

Furthermore, on this note, if things continue as they have, it seems likely that when our children marry, they will own homes debt free and have their colleges paid off or largely paid off. As such, they will be in positions to help their younger brothers and sisters. I am helping them accomplish these goals and they in turn will be freed up to help the next generation of younger ones. We're all in this together.

Like I said, it's not something I planned, but I discovered the benefits of this when David, my oldest, was about 12 and have stuck to it all these years. There is something about getting up in the morning and delivering newspapers and knowing that you are helping your family that is somehow not only very satisfying, but also produces a maturity beyond one's years. It's also called doing what we have to in order to make it all happen. I can't even say this is a biblical pattern or something to implement in your family, but it's what we did.

It's kind of funny when we think about it. When we explained to 12 and 14 year olds how much we were paying in interest per month, they would have given us their birthday money to help us get out of debt. Sharing our finances and communicating family goals gave us all purpose and unity and then high fives and reasons to celebrate as we began accomplishing them. The results have been quite serendipitous.

Rest Chapter Six

One might wonder why a chapter on rest would be included in a book on spirituality and family issues. The answer is because rest is not only critical to being healthy and successful, but also because it is something that our contemporary culture greatly struggles with. We are a culture of excesses and abuses in nearly everything we do and rest is not an exception.

I can't tell you how many people I have met, as well as acquaintances and friends whom we know, who have difficulty getting a good night's sleep. It is a real problem. Failure to get a good night's sleep affects everything we do. It decreases our productivity at work. It makes us grouchy. It alters the way we interact with others because we evaluate our activities based on how and when we can get a good night's sleep. It affects us when we travel because we are even more concerned with the quality of our sleep as we go to hotels, stay with relatives, or try to enjoy ourselves on vacation. Some people experience an entire night of disturbing sleep and wake up un-rested and miserable. I have seen this to be a great problem and something that must be overcome. Paul Harvey recently informed us that Americans fill 42 million prescriptions for sleeping pills and most experience fatigue the following day. This problem is huge.

On the other hand, others can get by on very little sleep and feel refreshed. Thomas Edison, Benjamin Franklin, George Washington, and Winston Churchill were those who could get by with three to five hours sleep and maintain incredible productivity and creativity.

Getting a good night's sleep and waking up feeling rested is essential to being healthy and productive and maximizing our activities and involvements. Let's not minimize the importance of this. Consider that if we sleep 8 out of 24 hours in a day, that's one third of our lives! If we consider that what takes place during these hours greatly affects the other 16 waking hours it takes on even more significance. Imagine also what it would be like if we could reduce this time by two hours per night and feel even more rested! Think of the possibilities! We could increase our enjoyment of our lives immensely and have time to do some of those things that we long to do but never seem to have the time for.

People often say to me "I don't know how you do all that you do." I do have a lot going on. I run a business with the full activities related to numerous employees, customers, and vendors including everything from sales and marketing to sweeping up and even an occasional junket scuba diving in the attic insulation chasing down roof leaks. I juggle activities with 12 kids and their numerous and varied involvements including everything from dentist appointments, sporting events, music lessons with concerts and recitals, and of course home schooling. We garden extensively, growing and processing most of the food that we will consume in a year. We enjoy skiing, playing hockey and soccer, and of course visiting with friends. We have several horses and chickens and in the past have had cows and sheep and, although I hate to admit it, goats too. Most of our lives we have attended church three to five times per week including early morning men's meetings and special board meetings. I enjoy reading and try to read at least five to ten pages per day in addition to my daily Bible reading. I also try to enjoy an occasional game of golf or pick up a brush and take a whack at oil painting and now I've taken up a little writing. I usually rack up a decent cell phone bill monthly so extensive conversations with friends and relatives out of state is an additional involvement that I enjoy. No wonder my wife thinks I am ADHD! Where do I get the time and energy to do all these things? From proper time management and rest. Is this unique to me, hereditary, or can productivity and restfulness be learned?

I have 12 children and all of them is a very sound sleeper. In fact, like me, they can sleep anywhere, anytime, and wake up feeling very rested. My family sleeps so soundly, at times it is literally impossible to wake them. This is no exaggeration. I believe that it is a gift from the Lord, but also a result of choices that we make and the lifestyle we lead. This has allowed us to do a lot as a family since we can drive all through the night in a crowded Suburban and arrive the next morning at a destination and conduct our business. We can at times work until 4 a.m. and sleep for three or four hours and put in another productive day. Our testimony is that rest and sleep have been very problem free and as a result the quality of our lives has been greatly increased.

In this chapter we will look at rest in four areas: Spiritual Rest, Emotional Rest, Intellectual Rest, and Physical Rest. The order of these is important since, like a pyramid, they build upon each other.

SPIRITUAL REST

The passage that we looked at earlier in Exodus provides some amazing insights.

> 12 And Moses said unto the LORD, see, thou sayest unto me, bring up this people: and thou hast not let me know whom thou wilt send with me. Yet thou hast said, I know thee by name, and thou hast also found grace in my sight.
>
> 13 Now therefore, I pray thee, if I have found grace in thy sight, shew me now thy way, that I may know thee, that I may find grace in thy sight: and consider that this nation is thy people.

14 **And he said, my presence shall go with thee, and I will give thee rest.**
15 And he said unto him; if thy presence go not with me, carry us not up hence.
16 For wherein shall it be known here that I and thy people have found grace in thy sight? Is it not in that thou goest with us? So shall we be separated, I and thy people, from all the people that are upon the face of the earth.
17 And the LORD said unto Moses, I will do this thing also that thou hast spoken: for thou hast found grace in my sight, and I know thee by name.
18 And he said, I beseech thee, shew me thy glory.
19 And he said, I will make all my goodness pass before thee, and I will proclaim the name of the LORD before thee; and will be gracious to whom I will be gracious, and will shew mercy on whom I will shew mercy.
20 And he said, Thou canst not see my face: for there shall no man see me, and live.
21 And the LORD said, Behold, there is a place by me, and thou shalt stand upon a rock:
22 And it shall come to pass, while my glory passeth by, that I will put thee in a cleft of the rock, and will cover thee with my hand while I pass by:
23 And I will take away mine hand, and thou shalt see my back parts: but my face shall not be seen. –Exodus 33:12-23 (KJV)

What an incredible passage. It's foundational in many ways because for the first time in human history, God promises in a special way to demonstrate his presence among a people. There is a crying out for a manifestation of God's presence and to know God's ways. What is the first promise from the mouth of God in response to this prayer? I will give thee rest. Wow!

What an insight into the needs of the human heart. Of all the possible manifestations of God's presence, namely his power, his peace, his blessing, his insights, his wisdom, his knowledge, of all these, the priority promise is rest. What does this tell us about our hearts and the needs of our souls?

I was recently relaxing on a cold January day. It was 20 below zero – back home. I was enjoying a breezy 85 degrees, taking in the sun and doing a little people watching. "It doesn't get any better than this," I thought to myself. I found a strategic spot to position myself as I watched thousands of white, overweight, over-pampered, overfed, westerners, mostly Americans, make their way off the pier of the cruise ship and down into the market square of this tropical, third world paradise that awaited them. The travelers were among the wealthiest people in the world. They were fulfilling dreams of luxury and personal fulfillment that most people on this planet only dream about. They were engaging in an activity that they had planned for and saved for most likely for the better part of a year or longer. Yet in spite of all this, their lives communicated tension and pain. I felt like walking up to some of them and saying "Smile, you're on vacation!" or "Please remind your face you're having a good time!" There were husbands and wives that were obviously at great odds with each other. I saw parents dragging crying kids through the square who were doing the typical Wal-Mart wiggle "Why CAN'T I have one of those mom" much to the consternation of the exasperated parents. Of course there was no shortage of singles who, although sporting a professional and imported tan from the local salon back home, betrayed their "I've got it all together" persona by the loneliness evident in their eyes and searching looks.

The Beatles had it figured out in their pop song with the lyrics that said, "I don't care too much for money, money can't buy me love… can't buy me love, love, yeah, yeah, yeah." The sad fact is that money and expensive vacations can't buy me rest and peace.

These people should have been the happiest people in the world! They had been eating the best food and partaking in pleasurable and leisurely activities, but it didn't satisfy. It didn't bring inner peace and rest. I spoke briefly with a young collegiate from Europe. Where was she off to? A Yoga class. There you have it, professional relaxation classes. The old TV series was appropriately named, "The Young and the Restless." Why is this the case?

True rest and peace begins as a product of one's spirit.

We are spiritual beings and rest is a gift imparted to us by our Creator. The word rest in Exodus is the word shabat. We get the word Sabbath from it. It's a picture of peace, balance, harmony, and equilibrium. It is the absence of stress, tension, labor and strenuous activity. The peace of God! One can have all manner of blessings and worldly possessions and not have the rest and peace of God.

One of the verses that has long intrigued me is Proverbs 20:22—"The blessing of the Lord maketh rich, and addeth not sorrow with it." Only God can give us the ability to enjoy our lives. I remember reading back in the 80s about Andy Gibb, one of the members of the BeeGee's who at 25 to 30 years old, good looking, wealthy, and famous died of an overdose, alone, in his hotel room.

On the other hand, visiting a third world country and finding some of the happiest people in the world who are without even the most basic of human necessities, but who love God with all their hearts, reveals the source of spiritual rest: fellowship with our Creator. How do we achieve this?

Most readers who've made it this far already have settled the issue of peace with God. It is the issue of salvation or deliverance from the power and penalty of sin. In a nutshell it is the surrendering of one's life to the Creator. Without this, one will never experience true rest and peace. The facts are quite simple.

Man is a sinner. Sins are the offenses against our Creator, our fellowman, and ultimately too, against ourselves. We have a natural inclination to selfishness and we need a savior, someone to deliver us from the power of our selfish inclinations, and from the ultimate penalty of them. That Savior is Jesus Christ! He is the perfect man who alone can usher us into the rest of God. The key word for us in this account is surrender. Have you surrendered your life to the Creator, Jesus Christ and received his free gift of forgiveness? If you haven't this is the critical need of your life today. But it can't stop there.

Being a Christian doesn't guarantee one a life of rest and peace. Why do so many believers fail to experience the rest of God? The writer to the Hebrews challenges us with this problem in a most fascinating way.

1. **Let us therefore fear, lest, a promise being left us of entering into his rest, any of you should seem to come short of it.**
2. For unto us was the gospel preached, as well as unto them: but the **word preached did not profit them, not being mixed with faith in them that heard it.**
3. **For we which have believed do enter into rest**, as he said, As I have sworn in my wrath, if they shall enter into my rest: although the works were finished from the foundation of the world.
4. For he spake in a certain place of the seventh day on this wise, And God did rest the seventh day from all his works.
5. And in this place again, If they shall enter into my rest.
    –Hebrews 4:1-5 (KJV)

Here we see the enigma of possessing something, but failing to partake of its practical presence in our lives. This is what happened to the Israelites. They were promised a "promised land," but many did not get to enter into the promised land. Why is that? The Scripture tells us that they did not because of their unbelief. They failed to believe God on the specific account. When it came down to the obedience of faith, they failed to obey and therefore did not experience the blessing of God.

So it is with believers. We can come short of it. We can fail to experience it. This failure cannot be on the part of God. It cannot be a lack of his supply. Failure on this part has to be something that we are doing wrong. On this account we are exhorted to exercise diligence. Sounds paradoxical; we need to work hard to rest! I believe the writer is saying, "Make sure you don't do anything to hinder the rest of God from being experienced in your life." Like guests on the cruise ships, are our churches any different? Has the church demonstrated to the world a lifestyle of rest that actually provokes the world to jealousy? Is there a peace, poise and calmness that characterizes our lives and our conversation that evidences that we have entered into his rest? Or do we live from crisis to crisis and somehow seem to have failed to enter into it?

We must realize that entering into God's rest will not come easy. An entire generation of Israelites perished without entering in. Many believers fail to experience the blessings of God that usher us into rest. The Israelites had to wage a war with the inhabitants of the land. It as a difficult task for them to fulfill. We too, as New Testament believers have to work hard to experience it. There are several things we must do if we are to experience God's rest, which begins with spiritual rest. There are three things that are absolutely necessary for entering into God's rest and experiencing subsequent physical rest. Fail in any one area and a restful life will be traded for one of anxiety, fear, tension, and distress. Let's take a look.

1. Maintain a clear conscience through confession of any known sin.

Although I've touched on this in Chapter 1, nowhere are the implications of this more evident than in the turmoil associated as a byproduct of unconfessed sin. Notice David's words:

> 1 Blessed is he whose transgression is forgiven, whose sin is covered.
> 2 Blessed is the man unto whom the LORD imputeth not iniquity, and in whose spirit there is no guile.
> 3 When I kept silence, my bones waxed old through my roaring all the day long.
> 4 For day and night thy hand was heavy upon me: my moisture is turned into the drought of summer. Selah.
> 5 I acknowledged my sin unto thee, and mine iniquity have I not hid. I said, I will confess my transgressions unto the LORD; and thou forgavest the iniquity of my sin. Selah. –Psalm 32:1-5 (KJV)

The spiritual and physical consequences of sin are obvious and multitudinous. Guilt, remorse, regret, fatigue, tension, anxiety, paranoia, and anger, are some dynamics of our spirit that result from unconfessed sin. These spiritual conditions can lead to insomnia, worry, heart disease, digestive disorders, anxiety diseases including bulimia and anorexia, rage, tension headaches, migraine headaches, grinding of one's teeth, jaw and dental problems, vision problems, asthma, allergies, and various autoimmune diseases. These can also lead us to coping strategies like overspending, overeating, and various indulgent behaviors.

Notice that the solution for David was confession. *I acknowledged my sin unto thee and mine iniquity I have not hid.*

To confess our sin is simply "to agree with God" about the sinfulness of our sin. This is the first step. Stop fooling yourself. Stop hiding it. Stop procrastinating about it and speak it out loud. "Lord this _____ is bad and I hate it. I agree it's wrong and it's an offense to you and it's wrecking my life. Take it from me. Help me to rid myself of it. At least make me willing to forsake it as you give me grace." This is the first step, agreeing with God concerning the sinfulness of my sin. When we do this, God moves in our lives with healing grace and forgives the iniquity of our sin.

Iniquity is an interesting term. How does God forgive the iniquity of our sin? We think sin committed is done in isolation of everything else in our lives. When former president Clinton was being impeached for immorality and lying to congress, the great discussion was "what he does in his personal life is his own business, as long as it doesn't interfere with his job." This was the wisdom of the world offered up wholesale by the media. The problem is that it isn't true. Iniquity is the intermingling of sins and the interrelationship of sins. It all fits together and affects the whole. Many sins work together to create entanglement. This is the nature of sin. This is why many people cannot break free from sin. They do not understand how one sin way over here in one little area of their life is creating bondage way over here in another area. Sins work together like links in a chain all wrapped around us. The more of them we cut, the quicker the chains fall to the ground. They lose their hold on us as we confess them. The power of their interrelations is diminished as we confess.

Let's illustrate. The guy goes to the bar because he is empty inside and wants to have a good time. While there he indulges in alcohol. With his inhibitions diminished he chain smokes. His eyes lust after the girl down at the end of the bar. He wants to impress her so he buys the whole place a round of drinks and overspends. He then leaves the bar and heads home only to lie to his wife and says he only stopped in for a few. All these sins have entangled themselves around him and he is caught in a world of iniquity.

Let's look at the ladies. She's feeling empty inside so she makes her way over to the refrigerator and throws a pizza in the oven and settles in to the steamy soap opera or movie. As the weight comes on she feels worse about herself and decides to go shopping because "I owe it to myself," and besides she does need some new clothes. While there she overspends and buys some things she really didn't need, but they were on sale. This leads to a big fight with her husband who can't understand why she's gaining so much weight and her spending is out of control. She feels unloved and the friends in the "chat room" seem more interesting than ever. She is caught in a world of iniquity.

In both cases, sins compound together to increase their effectiveness against them. When we confess our sin, God releases sin's grip upon us and enables us to break free. Will either one of these people ever experience the rest of God? It's doubtful.

Now we must notice something of great significance here. The principle stated says that we must confess *any* known sin. This is where the diligence comes in. We can allow little sins (if there were such things) to creep in, little offenses, and thus cut off the flow of rest and peace that God intends for us.

Sometimes when it comes to sin we seem to think, "What we don't know won't hurt us." In other words, if a sin is growing outside the backdoor of our lives and it's just a little one, it's okay, because "it only affects me and it doesn't bother anybody." The truth is that it does. I remember one hot July day I was taking a two hour trip, running an errand, down and back to St. Cloud. I had a fun little Toyota with a five speed. After driving big vans and pickups driving that Toyota was like running a go-cart. I was having a blast zipping in and out of the metro traffic and sitting four inches off the asphalt. Little did I know, the engine was running hot. About a few miles from my home I discovered that the temperature needle was pegged. The damage was already done. The next day the motor was smoked. I totally missed the early warning system. While I was tooling around enjoying myself, the seeds of destruction were already at work. But it was only a little gauge! Only a little red needle! How could it do so much damage? That's the way it is with sin. Remember the proverb that says "It's the little foxes that spoil the vine."

Before we leave this concept I would not want the reader to feel hopeless at this point and thinking "Well, if I have to become sinless to experience the rest of God, I can forget it." It's more of a quantitative thing. The more we experience spiritual wholeness, the more rest we will avail ourselves of. Obviously some truths when violated have larger consequences than others. Our goal though is diligence to enter in. Let's look at the next road block to rest.

2. Forgive anyone who has sinned against you

The first hindrance dealt with our relationship with God; this second one deals with our relationship with our fellowman. Jesus' teaching in Matthew 18 speaks to this issue.

> 21 Then came Peter to him, and said, Lord, how oft shall my brother sin against me, and I forgive him? Till seven times?
> 22 Jesus saith unto him, I say not unto thee, until seven times: but, until seventy times seven.
> 23 Therefore is the kingdom of heaven likened unto a certain king, which would take account of his servants.

24 And when he had begun to reckon, one was brought unto him, which owed him ten thousand talents.
25 But forasmuch as he had not to pay, his lord commanded him to be sold, and his wife, and children, and all that he had, and payment to be made.
26 The servant therefore fell down, and worshipped him, saying, Lord, have patience with me, and I will pay thee all.
27 Then the lord of that servant was moved with compassion, and loosed him, and forgave him the debt.
28 But the same servant went out, and found one of his fellow servants, which owed him an hundred pence: and he laid hands on him, and took him by the throat, saying, Pay me that thou owest.
29 And his fellow servant fell down at his feet, and besought him, saying, Have patience with me, and I will pay thee all.
30 And he would not: but went and cast him into prison, till he should pay the debt.
31 So when his fellow servants saw what was done, they were very sorry, and came and told unto their lord all that was done.
32 Then his lord, after that he had called him, said unto him, O thou wicked servant, I forgave thee all that debt, because thou desiredst me:
33 Shouldest not thou also have had compassion on thy fellow servant, even as I had pity on thee?
34 And his lord was wroth, and delivered him to the tormentors, till he should pay all that was due unto him.
35 So likewise shall my heavenly Father do also unto you, if ye from your hearts forgive not every one his brother their trespasses. –Matthew 18:21-35 (KJV)

This is an interesting and incredible parable. Perhaps we've all heard it before and it merits our study and attention. There are many lessons we need to learn from this and I comment it to the reader's study. However I wish only to focus on one verse, verse 34.

Notice the result of the lack of forgiveness on this slave. The Lord in this parable is the LORD, our God. The point is that he forgave the slave of a huge debt and the slave was unwilling to forgive his fellow slave of a relatively insignificant debt in comparison. The judgment pronounced on him in verse 34 is astounding. Notice that he was "delivered over to the tormentors." This is interesting. Who were these tormentors? Why would God do such a thing?

I believe that God does exactly that when we fail to forgive our fellow man. He turns us over to the tormentors. Who are they? They are the tormentors of our souls including, resentment, animosity, bitterness, grief, revenge, and the list could go on and on. These lead to the complete list of physical symptoms enumerated above that rob us of health and rest. Rest will never be ours if we harbor resentments and fail to forgive others.

Additionally, when we fail to forgive we invite Satan's attack against us. Ephesians 4:26 tells us "Do not let the sun go down on your anger and do not give 'place' to the Devil." When we fail to forgive and hold grudges we give Satan ground in our lives to set up an enemy camp and from there to rob us in a thousand ways of the rest we so desire.

Take a complete inventory—parents, teachers, brothers and sisters, extended family members, co-workers and supervisors—if there is anyone whom you are holding a grudge against, you've got to let it go. It's only destroying you. But how do we practically do this?

Whenever we fail to forgive someone we hold them responsible for a debt that they owe us. They did something to us, or failed to do something for us, and as a result they owe us. It could be monetary. It could be emotional; it could be the loss of something like an opportunity that cannot be replaced. Whatever it is there is a debt that we feel that they owe us. The first step is to realize what it is that we feel they owe us. The second step is to release the person from this debt. Let them go. Tell them in your mind that you no longer require it of them (whether you do this literally, in person, is something you will need the Lord to give you guidance about).

There is usually an emotional debt to pay. This requires that you be willing to bear the emotional pain of this offense *for the rest of your life without ever bringing it up again.* There is a price to pay and forgiveness means that *I will be willing to pay it as often as necessary.* Every time that offense comes up I am going to pay the price and give the offense and my broken emotions to Jesus.

This is a foundation to experiencing spiritual rest, namely, peace with God and peace with others. Let's look at the third foundation.

3. Become thoroughly convinced of God's love for you.

Our minds can really be twisted things. We can get so caught up in false guilt, feeling inferior, feeling unwanted, feeling lonely and unloved, and feeling useless. It's easy to become restless and filled with all manner of emotions and the psychosomatic ailments that result from these feelings. Believers are not exempt. Most of the trouble we get ourselves into are a result of feeling unloved by God and by others. Conversely the greatest power in the world is the power of being and knowing that one is loved. Just about anything in the world can be going wrong around you and if you know you are loved, you can get through it.

Romans 8:37-39 speaks to this issue.

37 Nay, in all these things we are more than conquerors through him that loved us.

38 For I am persuaded, that neither death, nor life, nor angels, nor principalities, nor powers, nor things present, nor things to come,

39 Nor height, nor depth, nor any other creature, shall be able to separate us from the love of God, which is in Christ Jesus our Lord. (KJV)

We conquer through love! We overcome all of our circumstances because we realize that God loves us! Nothing can separate us from his love! That is amazing! He loves us unconditionally. Romans 5:8 tells us that God demonstrates his love toward us, in that, while we were yet sinners, Christ died for us. He loved us while we were sinners. He saw us in all of our sin and the mess that we were making of our lives and he chose to love us anyway. He didn't wait until we got our act together and brought our lives together to some level of sinlessness. He loved us while we were sinners. He knows every sin we would ever commit, past, present, and future and he loves us anyway. This is so freeing!

Notice now Romans 8:31, "If God be for us who can be against us?" What an incredible concept. The Creator of the universe, the Lord of Hosts, the God of Abraham, Isaac, and Jacob, the Everlasting God is on MY side. He is for me and not against me. He is there to help me. He knows all my faults and sins and shortcomings and still wants to meet me with his tender mercy and kindness!

With this understanding guiding our lives we can live in freedom and ultimate spiritual rest. Practically, this means several things:

- I'm okay because God doesn't make any mistakes.
- God loves me and will never leave me or forsake me.

- God knows what I am going through.
- I can handle anything that comes my way because he monitors everything that across my path.

Wow! With this sound foundation in place we can experience spiritual rest and now we are ready for emotional and physical rest.

EMOTIONAL REST

Emotional rest is the absence of inner turmoil in one's spirit and relationships. It deals with our relationship with ourselves, our self concept and our relationship with others. It begins with an understanding that I'm okay. It involves an understanding that God is working in and through all the things in my life over which I have no control. Someone has once described the difference between worry and concern as "care over something concerning which we have no control." Much of our emotional unrest results from not coming to grips with those things in life that are beyond our control. Consider the following things that often cause us emotional unrest.

1. Our family and ancestry.

We cannot control the family we were born into. We didn't choose it. God permitted it to happen and of all the families in the world he allowed us to be in the one we found ourselves in. Family dysfunction is a "normal" part of existing in a fallen world. As someone once said, "Normal is merely a setting on my washing machine." Were your parents divorced? Did you experience poverty? Abuse? Neglect? Unstable parents? Perhaps you were adopted. Often times these residual feelings of unresolved conflicts of our youth and the resultant emotional turmoil continue to wreak havoc well into our adult lives. Following this enumerated list of unchangeable events in our lives I will suggest some healing solutions.

2. **Our personality and birth order.**

These things can be related. We are wired a certain way. Some of us are outgoing and others are more quiet, reflective, and analytical. Although we can grow in character and maturity, we cannot change our basic personality traits. Coming to grips with this will bring emotional healing as we learn to accept our strengths and weaknesses. This is often related to birth order in that often times our birth order enhances our personality types. For example firstborns are often more responsible and driven. Second-borns are often competitive or even manipulative. Third-borns and subsequent birth orders can be more sanguine or easy going. Understanding the dynamics of our nuclear family and how the effects of birth order interact with our personalities can be insightful. Understanding this is the first step to emotional rest and sometimes untangling the internal emotions of why we feel the way we do in certain situations, and why we do the things that we do.

3. **Our physical frame and health make up.**

God in his wisdom created each of the nearly 6 billion people on the face of this planet all different. Some are tall, some short. Some are thin, and some are large. Some have lots of hair, some have little or none. Some have all their limbs, some do not. Some have above average intelligence, others have mental handicaps. Some have dark skin, some have light skin. The fact of the matter is that we did not choose our physical make up and outside of drastic efforts or severe surgery we usually cannot change it. This is something that affects us the whole of our lives and can be a great source of emotional unrest, especially as we go through the changing seasons of life. We all age differently. Being at peace with ourselves as we contemplate our physical bodies is essential for emotional and physical health. Failure to do so can lead not only to emotional turmoil, but also to destructive and costly decisions later in life.

4. Our Gender.

I have to list this one separately, although it could be included in the above. For millenniums man has believed that God has created man male and female. All of that is being seriously called into question now days. The 'medicalization of deviance' has occurred today in that man in his so called wisdom has invented diseases to describe emotional confusion and wrong thinking about gender. Gender disorder, identity disorder, and a whole host of alternative lifestyles have resulted. Although proponents of these gender lifestyles promise freedom and healing, the fact remains that failure to accept the Judeo Christian historical position on these things will lead to a life of inner conflict, pain, confusion, loneliness, isolation, and in many cases premature death.

As we consider these unchangeable things and the huge impact they have on the emotional side of our personalities, how can we reconcile the difficulties that come to us through this venue? Once again we must allow our Creator to speak to us and bring healing.

Ephesians 2:10 is insightful. It says, "For we are his workmanship created in Christ Jesus for good works, which God prepared beforehand that we should walk in them." The word *workmanship* here is the key concept. It is the Greek word *poema*. We literally are a poem that God is writing. He has created us and is weaving all of these uncontrollable circumstances of our lives together for his glory. I know I'm special because "God don't make no junk." He is aware of every detail of our lives, every physical trait, infirmity, birth defect, personality quirk, you name it. He knows all of this and they actually become "God's marks of ownership" in our lives. He allows the complete combination of unique circumstances and physical characteristics to come into our lives to bring glory to himself and joy to ourselves. Let me illustrate.

While on vacation recently, I was watching a young boy with Downs Syndrome interact with his family. He was about five and absolutely hilarious and cute. He was surfing and having a ball. I thought about all the extra care required by his father and mother. I thought about all the extra care and understanding that were required of his brothers and sisters. As we drove home from our trip as a family I thought of all the comments from my kids as they watched this kid and what a good time he was having and what a blessing he was to all of us. I thought that it's this kind of thing that can cause devastation in a marriage and how these parents have come to emotional healing and have gotten beyond the pain and the blame and moved into the blessing. They saw the *poem* that God was writing in their lives and were enjoying the blessing of it.

Show me a person who has accepted themselves, likes themselves (in a healthy way), and who has allowed the Spirit of God to bring healing to all these areas of potential pain and emotional confusion, and I'll show you a person who is an oasis of rest and comfort in this hurting world.

As we move into physical rest, we have laid a foundation of spiritual rest, emotional rest, but first we must consider Intellectual refreshment.

INTELLECTUAL REFRESHMENT

One might find this a strange topic as it relates to rest. The facts are simple. God has created this three pound mass called a brain that occupies our cranial cavity as a fascinating tool for running and organizing our physical bodies and the direction of our lives. It has capacities that far exceed even the most powerful computers. If we are to experience rest, our minds must be properly engaged. We've all been there: 1a.m., 2 a.m., 3 a.m., we're lying in bed wide awake and our minds are ticking away. Our bodies are tired, our souls and spirits are perhaps drained, but our minds are wired and racing one hundred and ten miles per hour and we can't sleep. This can be a real problem.

I've titled this section *Intellectual Refreshment*, because I believe God has created us for intellectual stimulation and maximizing our intellectual intake and output. Let me explain. We need to have active minds which are fully engaged in the world of ideas. We need to be problem solving, growing, learning, and fully involved in growing in our intellectual capacities. Unfortunately this is not the case today.

We live in a world of amusement. The word amusement is from the root word "to muse or to think"; the "a'" in front if it means not. Amusement is literally, "not thinking or without thinking." We live in a culture of amusement. The constant watching of television has become an American way of life. Young people today are raised with Nintendo, Xbox, and an endless supply of video games and movies. It's not unusual today for the average American family to come home from school or work and watch three to seven hours of television before bed. I believe this lifestyle of continued amusements destroys our minds and leaves us restless and unfulfilled. Our minds process massive amounts of information without interacting with it. I believe these lifestyle habits are equivalent to swallowing food without chewing it. It fails to nourish us and satisfy us and creates digestive problems.

On the other hand our minds should be engaged in stimulating activities through reading and research. Reading a novel or historical biography provides exercise to an inquiring mind. After a hard day of work, reading unrelated subject matter such as sciences, history, geographical or cultural studies, or reading about hobbies stimulates the mind and brings fulfillment and fatigue required to sleep soundly. Activities such as quilting, painting, archery, and playing musical instruments provide intellectual stimulation necessary to fill our minds, relieve boredom, and create a healthy fatigue. I believe much of the restless today is largely related to our unexercised and lethargic minds.

My own practice is that I usually read every night until exhaustion sets in. This could be literally two to twenty minutes. I literally fight to stay awake because I truly enjoy what I am reading. When I can't keep my eyes open any longer I shut off the light and use the remaining few moments to reflect on what I was reading. I have no trouble sleeping. Intellectual refreshment is a critical foundation to experiencing physical rest. Let's take a look at physical rest now.

PHYSICAL REST

—How to get a good night's sleep

7. When you wake up, get up.

Getting a good night's sleep begins by waking up early. That's right. Waking up early is important because we eliminate un-useful and un-restful sleep that we often get in the morning after we wake up. We try to get more sleep after we wake up by trying to go back to sleep. This is a big problem because the quality of sleep we get does not leave us rested. Often we then oversleep, and wake up later than we wanted to, creating undue stress and angst. This leaves us restless the following night and we start the vicious cycle of staying up late and sleeping later. The longer and deeper this cycle gets entrenched, the worse we feel and the poorer our daytime performance becomes. There is a real simple solution. When we wake up, get up.

2. Work hard.

Ecclesiastes says, "Whatsoever thy hand findeth to do, do it with all thy might." We live in a society of tentativeness. Everyone wants to put their toe in the water and see how it feels. Try it out and see if I like it. This attitude invades everything we do from marriage to church involvement. There is little zest for life and passionate living today. People who do work hard today are often labeled as workaholics. The Scripture tells us in Ecclesiastes 5:12, "The sleep of a laboring man is sweet, whether he eat little or much: but the abundance of the rich will not suffer him to sleep" (KJV). When we work hard and enjoy our work we come away from it with a fulfillment and corresponding physical and mental exhaustion that welcomes a good night's rest. Hard work is a good formula for a good night's sleep.

3. Push it and stretch yourself.

As noted earlier, we really may not need 8 to 10 hours of sleep per night. After work or a full day's activities one might want to undertake some other meaningful activity. Personally I find a number of things to do in the evening hours that stretches my day, increases my productivity, and prepares me for a good night's sleep. After working a full day I might go to another job and work from 7 to 11 p.m., 12, 1, 2, or even 3 a.m.! Going to a different jobsite, engaging in tile or trim work and focusing on a completely different activity not only leaves me with a few extra dollars, it also leaves me quite tired and ready to literally hit the pillow. By the end of the day I may have worked 12 to 20 hours but I am not exhausted because I took a break in between jobs, did different activities, and found satisfaction in the accomplishments of both activities. As I hit the pillow, I am already looking forward to tomorrow because I've got a lot to do now in both places. My mind is satisfied because I accomplished an extraordinary amount of work and I will sleep like a baby.

Other times I might do some type of home improvement project that takes me until 11 or 12 at night. Some nights I might start a hobby like an oil painting at 9 p.m. and finish at midnight. I may be tired at ten o'clock but I push myself until midnight to complete a certain phase of it and by midnight I am ready for bed and grateful for the accomplishments of the past three hours, hours I may have wasted sleeping. When I finally do get to sleep, I don't wake up even once until morning where I usually wake up after four to six hours of a dead sound sleep.

4. When you can't sleep don't.

What do I mean by that? Not being able to sleep is an abnormal condition. At least we can say it's very unpleasant. I believe that if we can't sleep there must be a reason. Because I am a sound sleeper, if for some reason I can't sleep, God must have a higher purpose in it for me. I believe he is trying to tell me something. My body belongs to Him. My mind belongs to him. Three hundred and sixty days a year I sleep like a rock. The few days a year I find myself waking up at one, two, three, or four in the morning I start asking "Okay Lord, why have you woken me up? What do you have to say to me? What is it that you want me to be thinking about?" Often times I'll turn on the light and read for an hour or two. I might get up and pray or read the Word. I might get up and get a legal pad and write down the thoughts that are flooding into my mind. It has been times like these that I have received direction for living, insights into God's word, and solutions for issues I'm facing. Occasionally I'll wake up at three a.m. I know I should be sleeping. I only went to bed at midnight and I feel that I need more than three hours of sleep. So I try to go back to sleep. If I can't, I figure that God has a reason and a purpose and I get up and go into the office. Working from 3:30 until 7:30 a.m. can be incredibly rewarding. During these rare times I've gotten a half day's work done before my normal work day might start at seven or eight a.m. I've found that it's times like these that I really needed to get some extra work done. I have discovered that within days of these seeming "interruptions" some opportunity comes up and my overloaded schedule is cleared because I just got done a bunch of backlog thus freeing me up to take advantage of this opportunity. It's great to look back and see that it was indeed the Lord waking me up to get a bunch of stuff done so my responsibilities would be fulfilled in order to partake of an opportunity he was sending my way. Even in our sleep, and at times the lack thereof, is an opportunity to "walk with the Lord."

As we close this section on physical rest, again our testimony here is one of great blessing. I have raised 12 children who can sleep anywhere. We can enjoy vacations, traveling, missions opportunities and focus on the people and situations around us and not be preoccupied with our comfort or when or where we will sleep. We can even get a good night's sleep on the ground, hard gym floor, or even in a church pew (preferably not during church service).

One of my favorite hymns is "Jesus I Am Resting." I read the biography of Hudson Taylor and learned that it, too, was one of his favorite songs and the Lord allowed it to become so during a time of great trial in his life. He was responsible for the care and numerous details of over one thousand missionaries on the field of China's interior. He was for the first time in his life helpless and literally on his back in a hospital bed. There he lay for months staring up at the ceiling and these words became most precious to him.

> "Jesus I am resting, resting, in the joy of what thou art, I am finding out the greatness of thy loving heart. As thou bidst me gaze upon me as I seek the lost to win I am ever hoping, resting in thy loving heart".

In this time of distress, Jesus communicated His presence and sufficiency to him in a greater way and he was able to release the burden of the work to the Lord and experience great rest of spirit and abundant supernatural supply of spiritual strength and provision as he waited upon the Lord during that year of infirmity.

This concept has always been an important one to me. My first email address was *paulisresting*. Because I work so hard and am a Type A personality with lots of responsibilities and obligations, experiencing God's rest has always been a priority to me. It has truly been one of the great joys of my life as I have walked with Him all these years.

I hope these ideas will assist you in maximizing a life of rest and enhance your involvements and relationships as a result. May the Lord bless you and keep you and give you rest!

Conclusion: A Call to Action

Although this book is a collection of essays gathered around a common theme of faith, family, and personal success. I would like to close with a modern day prophecy or an application of an old prophecy from Isaiah Chapter three. In the chronology of all this, I have written this manuscript two full years ago. I laid it aside, waited, worked, and prayed for the Lord's timing to publish it. One interesting thing is that I never wrote an ending or conclusion, or summarizing synthesis. Now I see why as I contemplate the following prophetic interpretation.

The book is about fining joy, success, and happiness in a life in touch with our Creator. It has been about thinking creatively and in faith about many common spiritual concepts and Scripture passages and the Joy that can result from radical obedience. I hope it has been an encouragement as you have read and continue to reflect and apply these concepts to your life. In closing, at the risk of seeming negative, I would like to contrast the above chapters and ultimately a life of faith, with what we see happening all around us today in our culture of unbelief. First, lets briefly define that.

Without starting another book, let us simply recognize that this contemporary American culture is summed up by the term Postmodernism and is the antithesis of the life of faith. It espouses the following world views or value structures:

Naturalism: Only that which is of the natural process is real, believable, and verifiable. The Supernatural does not exist and man is left to natural selection and randomness. The result is despair.

Hedonism: Hedonism is the practical ethical out working of naturalism and is the idea that says "Whatever feels good, do it!" After all, if there is no God, (not even a Divine Mover, himself unmoved as one philosopher expressed it), then there is no basis for moral judgments and we are left to define morality completely for ourselves. We have seen what this has produced beginning in our history in the 60's with the sexual revolution. This has lead to no fault divorce, an absence of reproductive ethics in terms of birth control, abortion, and of course now complete madness with respect to those things which for ages have been so central to the human race. I am referring to gender identity, and the universal abhorrence of Sodomy, and bestiality. The best Richard Dawkins, the 'foremost leading atheist' can come up with is that morality is based on our altruistic genes, that we derive from our primate ancestors. How pathetic! The incongruity of this thinking so ridiculous it is literally pathetic. To on one hand say that the animal kingdom is a hierarchy of survival of the fittest class structure of evolution where the strong survive and the weak die and then to say that it's the loving and nurturing instincts that we possess as animals that lead us to moral greatness is ludicrous. The result is despair for two reasons. Man cannot outshout his conscience. As much as the gay rights folks want to blame the homophobic culture of humanity for the fact that the live in guilt and shame, they stand self accused. The second reason for despair with respect to morality is the results reaped in the lives of those who stray from the path of biblical morality. Their lives are simply a mess and the result is internal and external chaos and despair.

Totalitarianism: this is the antithesis of personal freedom. Whenever principles of biblical faith are violated in human relationships, and ultimately in the organizing principles of human government, anarchy and totalitarianism will likely be the results. This is what we are seeing in America today with the proliferation of thousands and thousands of laws and a legal system which is growing in complexity. Additionally it is becoming commonly understood that justice is only for those who can afford it. Consider the absurdity of my neighbor being fined $300 for pulling a weed out of her lake front by the water commission, or someone loosing their privilege to drive because they failed to wear a crash restraint belt. The insanity of the laws and the legal system and the bureaucratic red tape associated with doing anything are natural outcomes of the breakdown of society with respect to biblical values.

With these fundamental world views in juxtaposition with the a biblical world view, let us look briefly at an ancient prophecy from Isaiah Chapter three.

"Isaiah 3:8 For Jerusalem has stumbled, and Judah has fallen, because their speech and their actions are against the Lord
First, we see that a society falls when their actions and speech are against the Lord. Isn't it interesting that the advance of pornography laws and even child pornography are substantiated on the basis of free speech? This is so strategic for our day. So much evil and wrong thinking is perpetuated on the basis of free speech and civil rights. This is also corroborated by groups like Citizens United for the Separation of Church and State and the ACLU who have worked hard to remove the clear and undeniable foundation of the Bible and biblical values from the founding fathers lives and the documents that they wrote.

'The expression on their faces bears witness against them." Today we have more people suffering from depression and medicated from the older set to the preschoolers with ADHD on Riddlyn, and we have a national epidemic of addiction to prescription narcotics such as oxycotton and oxycodon. This is nearly as bad as the meth problem among street type illegal drug users. The countenances of our generation are bearing witness against them. Finding personal 'happiness and fulfillment' has run it's course and we are living with a culture of despair. Francis Schaeffer predicted this 20 years ago along it's implications to the church and his writings were were so prophetic we see it unfolding before our eyes. Let's continue in Isaiah.

"They rebel against the Lord and His Glorious presence... No other nation in the world apart form Israel was founded with the expressed purpose of worshipping the living God in freedom of conscience and spreading His Glorious Gospel to the heathen as America. The founding documents as well as the fathers lives themselves so profoundly testify to this it gives one goose bumps just to read about the faith and sacrifices of these stalwart men. What do we see today? Complete redaction of this "glorious presence' of God in our nations past. The ACLU, Citizens United For Separation of Church and State, and a host of humanist and educational elites have all but wiped out even the memory of our nation founded upon the principles of Judeao- Christian God and His great Revelation, the Holy Scriptures. This has been a significantly strategic plan of our opponent, and he is succeeding. Back to Isaiah...

Verse 9 "They display their sin like Sodom and do not even conceal it... Woe to them!" I don't think I even need to comment on this. It's so far gone in our country we can even be arrested for hate crimes and put away for homophobia. I was recently cited anonymously by the local city newspaper editor as a dangerous religious fanatic whose fanatical views need to be silenced lest our society be overtaken by religious wacko's not unlike the Taliban. It's the Gay's, lesbians, bisexual, and transgender (GLBT) community that are the truly enlightened of society. They have transcended hate and become the true people of love and acceptance inspiring humanity to new vistas of personal growth and achievement as they encourage our middle school students and high school students to explore gay sex, cross dressing, transgenderism, bisexuality, and sexual experimentation to determine 'who they are' and what pleasures best suit them. **Friends, who would have thought that the enemy would have succeeded in accomplishing this in our lifetime! His sense of strategy is amazing.** Bear with me as we finish the Isaiah prophecy

Verse 12 O my people, their oppressors are children." Did I read that right? Children are the great oppressors of this fallen society? That's right! It started back in the 60's when we embraced rebellion as a cultural value. It's not unusual since that time to see some teen smack his dad or mom around, never mind cuss them out. The Juvenile Justice system has exploded in our country and we have a whole generation of parents who don't know what to do with their kids. This my brethren is an amazing strategy. Now we've come full circle because the whole world sits by the TV and radio watching the next kids of our generation terrorize the whole nation with killing sprees at their local schools. Names like Columbine, Virginia Tech, and Red Lake, among hundreds of others have become national household names. (Red Lake and Virginia tech just in the past year and one right in my back yard!.) I live in rural MN and my neighbor at 17 was gang killed in the mine dump with baseball bats , knives, and they finally finished him off with a shotgun. I watched this whole community go though the trial as several of the towns kids were convicted for this heinous crime which was a result of peer pressure of kids and gang violence. The strategy is working... People are at a great loss to know what to do with their kids in many practical ways. I meet lots of young parents who actually put their babies and toddlers in the car and drive them around at night to get them to go to sleep every night. They are hostages within their own homes and there aren't even any guns!

But back to Isaiah as the verse ends…

Vs. 12 'Women rule over them." Now friends, I think I am to understand this as a consequence of JUDGMENT against a nation that has turned its back on God. Why is this significant? 1. It's because of the weakness of men that women are ruling. WHERE ARE THE MEN TODAY who will stand and fight? Women have taken over the market place as managers, supervisors, and even CEO's. Its a whole huge managerial trend that companies can get women to work harder for less money and they are far more loyal to the company and willing to do the companies bidding sometimes, rather than what's right. Here we sit on the eve of the first female presidential hopeful. Sure, call me a chauvinist bigot as well, but we are also seeing the incredible proliferation of female ministers, and even in what were 10 years ago evangelical churches. Now please don't misunderstand me and paint me with that broad brush because I am not an alarmist, conspiracy theorist, or reactionary. I do indeed affirm all of Scripture in that God has indeed gifted and uses women in many places and settings and I affirm all that is good and right, but we must understand this in the greater strategy of the enemy. Often he uses the good to circumvent the best. It's right here in this Scripture passage, my brethren, when women rise to a great level of leadership in a society and in churches, it's a judgment against that nation. The fact of the matter is that we need strong men to be leaders in our homes, churches, and in society. Decreasing male leadership an minimizing male roles is such a significant strategy and the enemy is winning.

You see, in terms of strategy, in each one of these critical areas he has succeeded in turning the wrong into the right, and that which is right into that which is wrong. Proverbs tells us…Woe to those who call evil good and good evil.

So dear reader, I want to ask you what are you seeing as strategically significant in your world? If the enemy can keep us busy with secondary issues and events he will be moving forward with his strategy. Distraction with secondary issues is his great decoy to side track the church from being salt and light while he is watching vigilantly to advance his causes.

I am currently watching the DVD Series A Band of Brothers, with my older teens and young adults. We're observing and learning from the lessons of warfare and what happens in the minds of men in their battle strategies and coping strategies. It's fascinating when we consider the importance of battle strategy. Unfortunately *we rarely think and act strategically* and as a result we win battles, but we are loosing the greater war, the culture war, the war for the kingdom and the war for society. What has the church at large been doing for the past 20 years to combat these things? What are you doing and what is your church doing that is *strategic* in terms of overcoming these cultural trends that are destroying families?

Part of the great problem is that the battles are often won by counterintuitive measures. Let me explain.

Counter intuitive means that it's against our normal and natural inclinations. What seems to work what we think will not work are actually opposite. For example, As a veteran I can tell you that while a patrol is coming in range the tendency is to want to take out the enemy as soon as we engage contact, to shoot from a distance. It's uncomfortable to wait until its absolutely scary to engage because the enemy has walked right upon us. That's how God often works. The whole story of Gideon is about counterintuitive measures to win the war. No, Gideon, we only need 300 men to win this battle. We're going to use pictures and torches, not swords. Indeed, an amazing strategy. Our God is a God of strategy.

The simple truths I've laid out here are not only a formula for happiness and blessing, but also a great battle plan. May the Lord bless each and every one of you as you seek to live a life of faith, pleasing to the Father. May you not only discover a life of serendipitous Joy, but may the Lord raise up through you an army of faithful soldiers who will also do great damage to Satan's kingdom.

Thank you for investing your time in this manuscript. Please feel free to stay connected with the Durocher Family Ministries. Your help and support of the messages of this manuscript are vitally needed. Visit us at www.Durocherfamilyministries.com.
God bless you as you seek Him in all Your Ways.